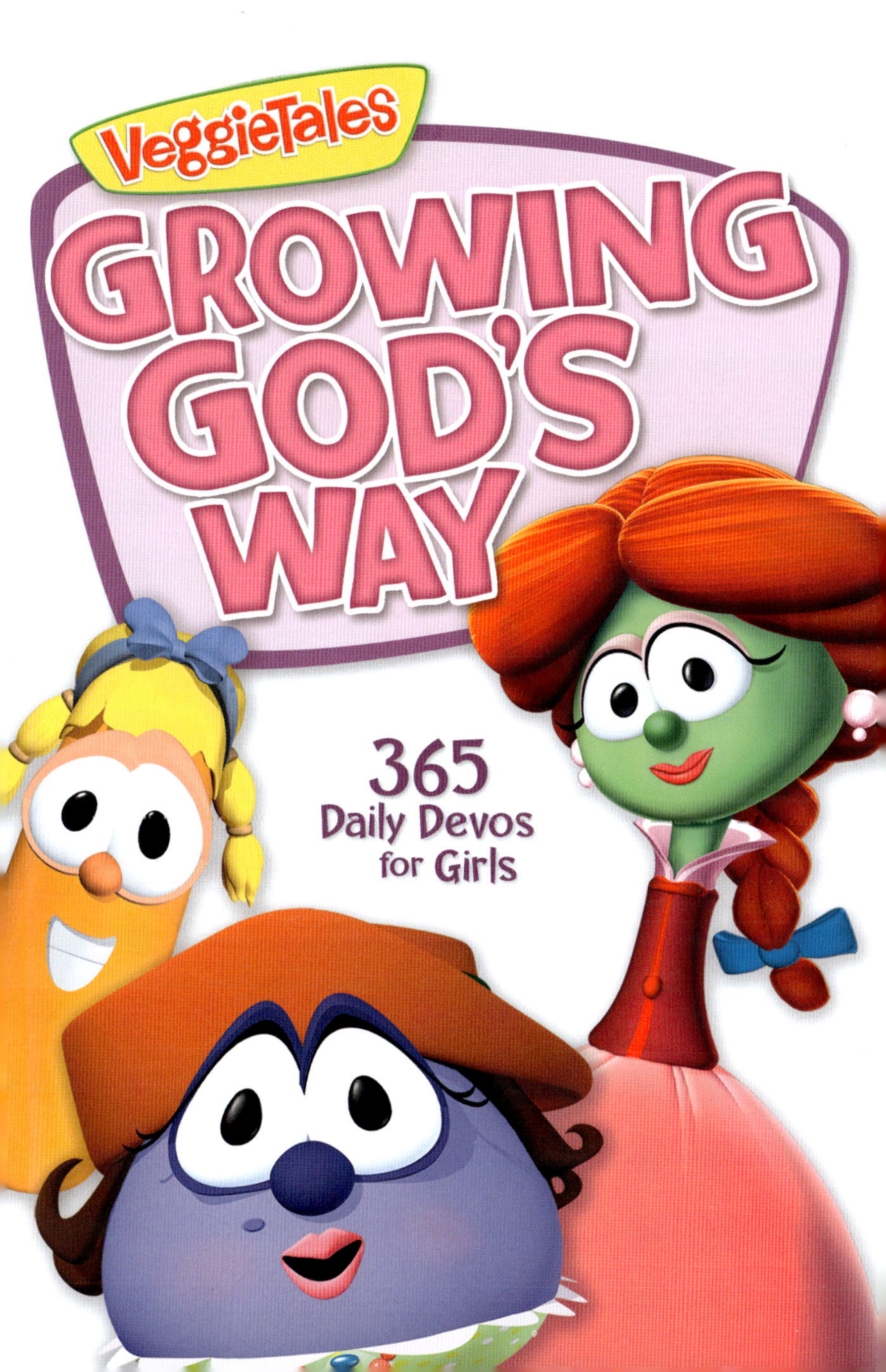
VeggieTales
GROWING GOD'S WAY
365 Daily Devos for Girls

veggietales.com

ISBN: 978-1-5460-0358-8 (paperback)
ISBN: 978-1-5460-0359-5 (padded hardcover)

WorthyKids
Hachette Book Group
1290 Avenue of the Americas, New York, NY 10104

WorthyKids is a division of Hachette Book Group, Inc. The WorthyKids name and logo are trademarks of Hachette Book Group, Inc.

Printed and bound in China
APS
10 9 8 7 6 5 4 3 2 1

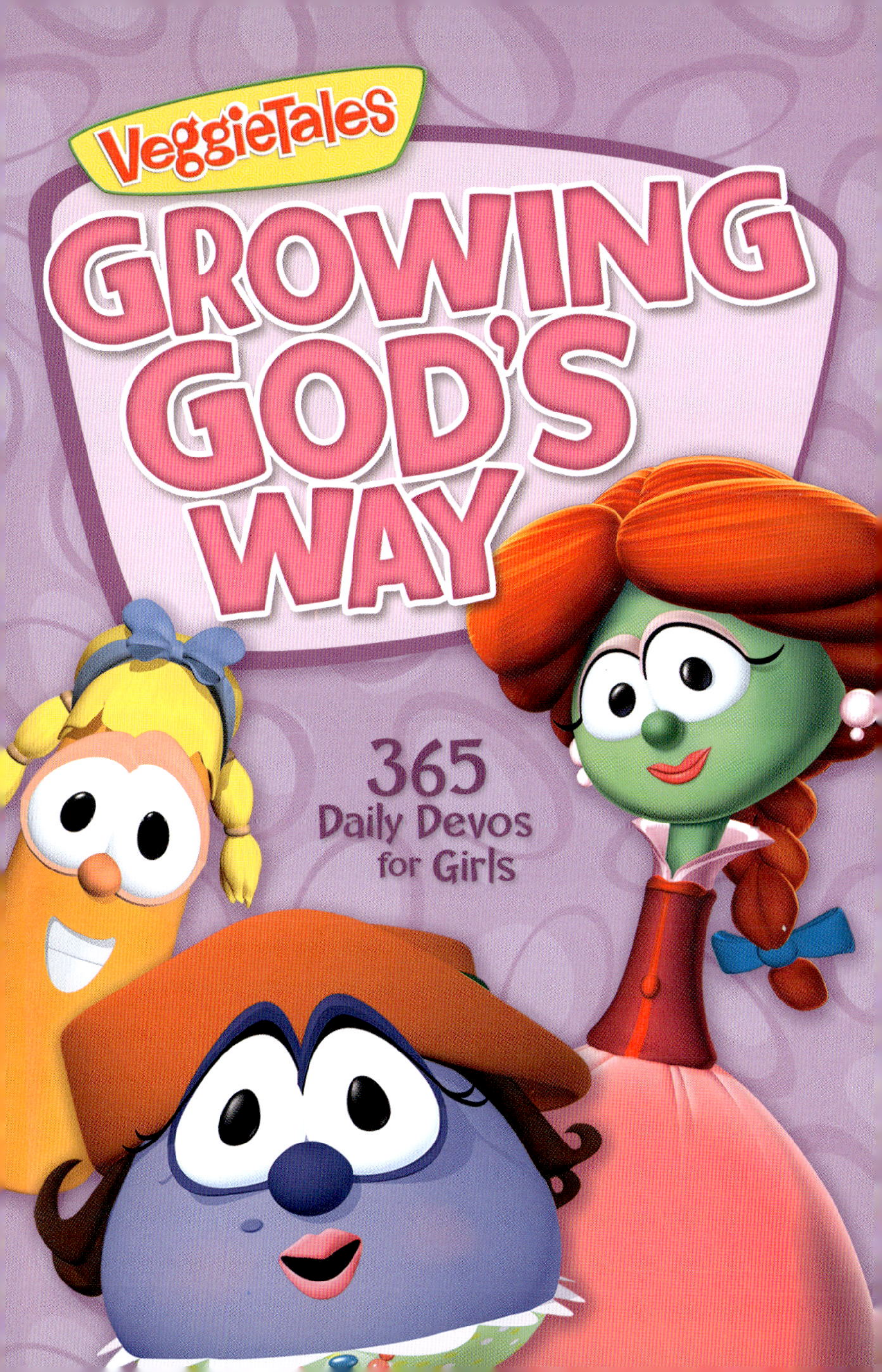
VeggieTales
GROWING GOD'S WAY
365
Daily Devos
for Girls

A NOTE TO PARENTS OR GRANDPARENTS

As a parent or grandparent, you know the importance of teaching children the big ideas that are found in God's Word and encouraging them to spend time with Him. The daily devotions in this book will help you do that.

Each entry contains a Bible verse and a kid-friendly devotion on an important topic such as honesty, forgiveness, or kindness. A question or thought follows to reinforce the message for the day, and a daily prayer will help your child to develop a habit of talking to God.

During the coming year, encourage your daughter or granddaughter to read a devotion from this book every day. This will help her establish a daily practice of hearing from God. It will also provide 365 opportunities to share God's love and wisdom and a daily chance for her to be reminded that God made her special—He knows her so well and loves her very much.

BE AN ENCOURAGER

You must encourage one another each day.

HEBREWS 3:13A CEV

If you are having a hard time or feeling sad, doesn't it feel great when someone comes along and cheers you up? Encouragement is a great gift we can give to each other. Sometimes we give encouragement with words like "I know you can do it" or "Keep on trying" or "I'm on your side." At other times, we don't even have to use words to encourage someone. A hug, a pat on the back, or just sitting with someone can be encouraging. You can find ways to encourage others every day—just give it a try!

THOUGHT OF THE DAY

Who will you encourage today?

PRAY TODAY

Dear Lord, Your loving care always encourages me. Please help me to find ways to encourage someone else today. Amen.

DAY 2

ONE STEP AT A TIME

All things should be done in the right way, one after the other.

1 CORINTHIANS 14:40 NLV

Sometimes, we all have to do things we don't like. It's easy to put off difficult or boring work until another day. But God can help us do what needs to be done, one step at a time.

Try to break a big (or boring) job into little pieces. Giving the dog a bath seems like a lot of work! But think about it in smaller steps like filling the tub, getting a towel, making soap bubbles, scrubbing your dog's belly, and cozy cuddles afterward! You only need to do one step at a time. Pretty soon, your work will be done!

THOUGHT OF THE DAY

When something hard needs to get done, smaller steps can make it fun!

PRAY TODAY

Dear God, when I have a big job to do, please help me find ways to make it seem easy and fun! Amen.

LAUGH TOGETHER

How we laughed and sang for joy. And the other nations said, "What amazing things the Lord has done for them."

PSALM 126:2 TLB

Have you ever been so happy you can't stop laughing? Sometimes a joke gives us the giggles. Sometimes a silly song or a goofy game will get you chuckling. Laughing can make a bad day good, and a good day even better!

God loves to hear us laugh. But it's a good idea to make sure everyone else is laughing too. If someone is left out or has hurt feelings, that's not very funny. It's never OK to laugh at someone. Instead, laugh with them! Find something that everyone agrees is silly. Then enjoy a good laugh, and a happy heart.

THOUGHT OF THE DAY

Larry loves to sing silly songs. Can you make up a silly song?

PRAY TODAY

Dear God, thank You for the gift of funny, happy times with my friends and family. What makes You laugh? Amen.

DAY 4

THE GIFT OF WORDS

How wonderful it is to be able to say the right thing at the right time!

PROVERBS 15:23B TLB

It's fun to give a gift that you know someone will enjoy. And one of the best gifts you can give is a kind word!

You can do so much with kind words. You can cheer up someone who is feeling sad. You can ask questions that show a friend you care about her. You can share a silly joke, or help a younger sibling learn something new. You can encourage someone who is having a hard time. Gifts aren't always big, expensive, or sparkly. Most of the time, the right words mean more than anything you could buy at a store!

THOUGHT OF THE DAY

Who can you give a "word gift" to today? What will you say?

PRAY TODAY

Dear God, thank You for my friends and family. Please show me the right words to say to each of them every day! Amen.

DAY 5

THE BEST FRIENDS

Look for the best in each other, and always do your best to bring it out.

1 THESSALONIANS 5:15 MSG

What makes a good friend? It's nice when you enjoy the same things, or can make each other laugh. But the most important thing friends do is to help each other be their best.

That might mean helping them finish a hard job. Or being excited when they win a big soccer game! It might also mean encouraging them to make good choices, even when it's not easy. Everyone makes mistakes—even friends. Don't give up on them! When you forgive each other and find ways to be kind together, you can all be your very best!

THOUGHT OF THE DAY

If you want the best friends, BE a best friend! What can you do to help a friend today?

PRAY TODAY

Dear God, thank You for my friends! Please show me how to bring out the best in each one! Amen.

GOD'S GREAT POWER

I pray . . . that you may know . . . incomparably great power for us who believe.

EPHESIANS 1:18–19 NIV

Have you ever wished that you could have a superhero by your side? Would it make you feel stronger or braver? Well, here's a secret: you do! You have God with you, and He is stronger and more powerful than any superhero you can imagine!

Nothing can make God stop loving you. No power on earth or in the heavens is greater than God. He made every star, and He keeps the planets in their places. He can help you solve any problem, and He can help you face any fear. God will never fail you!

THOUGHT OF THE DAY

God's power keeps you in His care, and He goes with you everywhere!

PRAY TODAY

Dear God, You are more powerful than any superhero. Thank You for loving me and taking care of me. Amen.

PEACE THAT LASTS

"You keep him in perfect peace whose mind is stayed on you, because he trusts in you."

ISAIAH 26:3 ESV

Do you ever have a hard time feeling peaceful? It's not always easy! But God offers peace that sticks around. All you have to do is trust Him.

God loves you. He knows everything, and He has good plans for you! He has promised He'll never leave, no matter what happens. So when you trust God, you don't have to worry about anything! Instead, you can feel peaceful, because you know God has everything under control. What could be better than that?

THOUGHT OF THE DAY

God's peace isn't hard to find. Just keep Him always on your mind!

PRAY TODAY

Dear God, thank You that I can find peace in You, no matter what happens! Amen.

DAY 8

LIVING IN LOVE

We know how much God loves us, and we have put our trust in his love. God is love, and all who live in love live in God, and God lives in them.

1 JOHN 4:16 NLT

How can you know God better? You can read your Bible and go to church. You can pray and spend time with Him! But don't forget one of the best ways to know God: live in love!

Living in love means that everything you do or say comes from a loving heart. Doing your chores without complaining is a good way to live in love. So is sharing your toys or standing up for someone who is being teased or left out. When you choose to act lovingly, you are growing closer to God. That's because God IS love!

THOUGHT OF THE DAY

You can love others best when you think about how much God loves YOU!

PRAY TODAY

Dear God, thank You for loving me so much. Please help me do everything with a loving heart. Amen.

POWERFUL WORDS

Be gracious in your speech. The goal is to bring out the best in others in a conversation, not put them down, not cut them out.

COLOSSIANS 4:6 MSG

What can you do with words? You can tell a joke, share an idea, ask a question, or calm someone down. Words can be really helpful! But if you're not careful, words can also hurt. They are powerful tools, and God wants you to choose them carefully.

So when you speak, ask yourself, "Will the things I say show God's love?" Gossip and unkind words make others feel angry or sad. But encouragement shows others that they are valuable and important. That's how God wants everyone to feel. So use your powerful words for good!

THOUGHT OF THE DAY

When kindness shines through every word, God is pleased with what He's heard!

PRAY TODAY

Dear God, I know that words have power. Help me use that power to share Your love with everyone! Amen.

DAY 10

MAKING CHOICES

I am offering you life or death, blessings or curses. Now, choose life! . . . To choose life is to love the LORD your God, obey him, and stay close to him.

DEUTERONOMY 30:19–20 NCV

How do you make a choice? Do you pick the petals off a daisy? Do you flip a coin? Do you ask someone to pick a hand? Did you know there is a much better way to make a choice?

The Bible says that when we love God, obey Him, and stay close to Him, He helps us make good decisions. We can stay close to God by reading His words in the Bible and by talking to Him in prayer. Then, when those tough choices come along, He'll show us the right thing to do!

THOUGHT OF THE DAY

Next time you have to make a tough choice, talk to God first. He loves to help!

PRAY TODAY

Dear God, every day is filled with choices. Will You please help me make good ones? Amen.

DAY 11

YOU HAVE SO MUCH!

"I came that they may have and enjoy life, and have it in abundance [to the full, till it overflows]."

JOHN 10:10 AMP

When you follow Jesus, your life is full! That doesn't mean it's full of things. You might not get every toy you want or go on every cool vacation your friends do. But you get to fill your days with wonderful gifts from God!

When you try something new, you have confidence God will help you. When you feel afraid, you have peace that God is there. You can get excited about tomorrow because God has great plans for you! You can celebrate today because He loves you with a huge love. What a great big life you have with Jesus!

THOUGHT OF THE DAY

What are some things you enjoy about your life?

PRAY TODAY

Dear God, thank You for my big life! You have given me such wonderful gifts! Amen.

GOD KNOWS YOUR NEEDS

And my God will supply every need of yours according to his riches in glory in Christ Jesus.

PHILIPPIANS 4:19 ESV

The Bible says that God will give His children everything they need. Sometimes people think that means that God will give them everything they want—like the newest toys, games, or clothes. Those things are fun to have, but the gifts God gives us are much more wonderful.

God gives us His love, peace, and joy. He blesses us with friends and family. He always listens to our prayers, and He's made big plans for us. God doesn't promise to give us everything we want, but He does provide everything we need. Be sure to tell God "thanks" today!

THOUGHT OF THE DAY

God always provides His best for His children.

PRAY TODAY

Dear God, thank You for loving me and providing all I need. Amen.

SPEAKING COURAGEOUSLY

"Be strong! Be courageous! Do not be afraid of them! For the Lord your God will be with you. He will neither fail you nor forsake you."

DEUTERONOMY 31:6 TLB

The Bible tells many stories about prophets. Prophets are men and women who told others about God. Sometimes people didn't believe the prophets or tried to hurt them. But God gave each prophet courage to tell the truth and do the right thing. Because of brave prophets, lots of people heard about God's love and came to believe in Him.

You might meet people who don't believe in God like you do. Ask God to give you courage to share the good news about His love. You can be just like the brave prophets in the Bible!

THOUGHT OF THE DAY

Have you ever shared God's love with someone new?

PRAY TODAY

Dear God, please give me courage to tell everyone about Your love! Amen.

DAY 14

HELPFUL FRIENDS

As iron sharpens iron, so people can improve each other.

PROVERBS 27:17 NCV

Have you ever helped a friend learn how to do something better? Has a friend ever helped you? Good friends encourage one another to learn new things, and they also help each other improve. When a friend is having a hard time learning to play a sport or understand a math problem, you can practice with them or give them some tips. If you are feeling upset or sad about something, a good friend will listen and try to understand. Being a good friend means caring enough about someone to help them learn and grow.

THOUGHT OF THE DAY

How has a friend helped you? How have you helped a friend?

PRAY TODAY

Dear God, thank You for giving me good friends. Please help me be a good friend too. Amen.

FOLLOWING GOD

Follow God's example, therefore, as dearly loved children.

EPHESIANS 5:1 NIV

Do you know that little ducklings follow their mother wherever she goes? If she jumps into the water, they jump in too. When she swims, they swim after her. Ducklings learn by following their mother and copying her. In the same way, the Bible says we should follow God's example. We are His dearly loved children, and He wants us to become more like Him. God wants us to learn to love one another, to be kind, and to become the people He created us to be! The closer we follow Him, the more like Him we will become.

THOUGHT OF THE DAY

What will you do today to follow God's example?

PRAY TODAY

Dear God, thank You for calling me Your dearly loved child. Please help me to try to be more like You every day. Amen.

DAY 16

WHAT'S YOUR ATTITUDE?

Make your own attitude that of Christ Jesus.

PHILIPPIANS 2:5 HCSB

Your "attitude" is the way you show what you are thinking. If you have a mean attitude, you show it by being unkind and saying rude things. If you have a happy attitude, you show it by finding things to be glad about and cheering up the people around you. The Bible says we should try to have the same attitude as Jesus. Jesus helped people. He prayed for others. He forgave those who were unkind. He shared what He had. Jesus had a loving and joyful attitude and His actions showed it. What will your actions show about your attitude today?

THOUGHT OF THE DAY

If you love Jesus and you know it, be sure your actions really show it!

PRAY TODAY

Dear God, please help me to have the same attitude as Jesus, so I will act in ways that show His love. Amen.

DAY 17

FOOLISH FIGHTERS

It's a mark of good character to avert quarrels, but fools love to pick fights.

PROVERBS 20:3 MSG

When you and a friend or family member disagree, what do you do? Some people love to argue, say mean things, or even hit each other! Did you know that the Bible says those people are fools?

When you disagree with someone, don't be a fool. Look for ways to solve your disagreements without fighting. Maybe you can take turns. Or maybe you can take a break from being around each other and then come back and try again later. Fighting never ends up well. Good friends don't want to hurt one another. They want to find peaceful solutions, then get back to having fun!

THOUGHT OF THE DAY

What are some ways you can keep from fighting with others?

PRAY TODAY

Dear God, when I feel like fighting, help me remember to think about what You would want me to do instead. Amen.

SHINE YOUR LIGHT

"You are the light of the world. A city situated on a hill cannot be hidden."

MATTHEW 5:14 HCSB

Did you know that people pay attention to what you do and say? Just like a light on a hilltop shows people where the hill is, the way you act shows others where your heart is. If you are being kind, helping, playing fair, and telling the truth, others notice. They know your heart is in the right place.

Being a good example is like shining a light for Jesus. He wants you to show others the right way to live, speak, and act. When others see your light, they can follow you to Him. So be a light wherever you go!

THOUGHT OF THE DAY

Don't forget to shine your light by doing and saying what is right!

PRAY TODAY

Dear God, I want others to see Jesus shining in me. Please help me to do and say good things. Amen.

PATIENT AND KIND

Love is patient, love is kind.

1 CORINTHIANS 13:4 HCSB

When is it easy to be kind? Probably when you feel happy, right? When you're playing with a friend or making cookies with Mom, kind words come quickly. But what about when someone at school hurts your feelings, or your little brother or sister interrupts your favorite show? You might feel like saying unkind words instead!

God asks us to show love all the time. That means choosing kindness, especially when it's hard. It takes extra patience to be kind when you're frustrated, but take a breath and ask God for help. He can give you the best words to say!

THOUGHT OF THE DAY

Kindness doesn't mean you ignore how you feel. Just try explaining your feelings calmly and patiently!

PRAY TODAY

Dear God, I'm glad Your love is both patient and kind. Help me show that kind of love to everyone in my life. Amen.

CHOOSING WISDOM

Wisdom is more precious than rubies. Nothing you could want is equal to it.

PROVERBS 8:11 NCV

If you could have anything in the world, what would you choose? When God asked King Solomon to choose whatever he wanted, he chose wisdom. That might seem strange, but Solomon knew that if he had all the money or fame in the world, but he wasn't wise, he would lose everything.

God says that we can have wisdom too! All we have to do is ask for it. The next time you have to make a hard choice, ask God to give you wisdom to choose what's best. He promises that He will!

THOUGHT OF THE DAY

What was a time when you had to make a hard choice? How did God help you?

PRAY TODAY

Dear God, thank You for offering me the gift of wisdom. Help me remember to ask You whenever I have to make a hard choice. Amen.

WHAT DOES GOD SEE?

Create in me a pure heart, God, and make my spirit right again.

PSALM 51:10 NCV

When we disobey God, we might feel yucky inside. But God can fix that! You can tell God what went wrong, and then ask Him to help you try again. It feels great when God sets things right in your heart.

God loves to see you make good choices. But He also knows that everyone makes mistakes. When you ask God for forgiveness, He is so excited! That shows you love Him and want to follow Him. God always forgives when you ask. Then He can help you grow in kindness, wisdom, and love.

THOUGHT OF THE DAY

Any time your heart feels sad, God can clean it and make you glad!

PRAY TODAY

Dear God, thank You for loving me, inside and out! Please help me keep a clean heart. Amen.

DAY 22

PATIENCE FOR ALL

Be gentle to everyone, able to teach, and patient.

2 TIMOTHY 2:24B HCSB

Has someone ever told you to be patient? Sometimes patience means waiting to do something that you want to do. But sometimes patience means taking your time and choosing gentleness. Being patient is one of the best ways to show God's love.

When you help a younger sibling learn something new, that's a great chance to be patient. When you get upset, but you choose kind words instead of angry actions, you're showing gentleness. And every time you put someone else first, you're sharing God's great love!

How can you practice patience today?

THOUGHT OF THE DAY

Patience takes practice, and practice makes perfect!

PRAY TODAY

Dear God, it's not always easy to be patient. Please help me practice, so I can share Your love! Amen.

DAY 23

GOD'S RULES

Practice God's law—get a reputation for wisdom.

PROVERBS 28:7 MSG

Do you have rules to follow at home? Maybe you have to go to bed at a certain time or set the table each night. And I'll bet you aren't allowed to kick or hit! Rules at home help keep everyone safe and happy.

God has also made rules that will keep you safe and happy. And just like rules at home, it takes practice to follow them well. What matters most to God is that you try. So if you make a mistake, just talk to God about what you can do differently next time. Then try again!

THOUGHT OF THE DAY

When you work to learn God's way, you'll get better every day!

PRAY TODAY

Dear God, thank You for helping me try again whenever I need to. I want to learn to follow all Your good rules! Amen.

THINK FIRST!

Enthusiasm without knowledge is not good. If you act too quickly, you might make a mistake.

PROVERBS 19:2 NCV

God loves for you to enjoy every day. He wants you to have a great time learning and growing and trying new things!

It's good to get excited. It's OK to have big feelings. But those are times it's easy to act too quickly and make mistakes. God says slowing down can help. Try thinking about what can happen next. If you grab a toy away from your little sister, how will she feel? If you run outside in the snow without a coat, will you be comfortable? Thinking first is always the best choice!

THOUGHT OF THE DAY

When you think before you act, you'll have more fun. Now that's a fact!

PRAY TODAY

Dear God, it's hard to slow down when I feel excited or upset. Will You please help me to think before I act and speak? Amen.

FINISH THE JOB

"Solomon, you must understand this. The Lord has chosen you to build the Temple as his holy place. Be strong and finish the job."

1 CHRONICLES 28:10 ICB

It is fun to start a project. You have great ideas and are excited to try them out. But after a while, the work sometimes seems hard or boring. You might be tempted to quit. But that's just the time to remember that God has promised to help you be strong! He can help you finish any tough job. Are you learning to dance or to play soccer? Don't give up when things are hard or when you feel like you aren't doing well. Be strong and finish the job. God loves to help you, even when you feel like quitting.

THOUGHT OF THE DAY

What work would you like God to help you finish?

PRAY TODAY

Dear God, I'm glad You give me work to do. Will You please help me finish what I start? Amen.

DAY 26

CELEBRATE DIFFERENCES

We have different gifts, according to the grace given to each of us.

ROMANS 12:6A NIV

The Veggies know that they are each special and they are each good at different things. Larry plays several musical instruments and makes up the silliest songs. Bob the Tomato is a great friend and loves to learn new things. Petunia is known for her kindness and Pa Grape is filled with wisdom. Just like the Veggies, each person has different likes, dislikes, talents, and interests. That's how God made us! It's important to thank God for our different gifts. They are all wonderful and worth celebrating!

THOUGHT OF THE DAY

What are some things that make you special and different from your friends?

PRAY TODAY

Thank You, God, for making each person special. Help me enjoy and celebrate the differences I see around me. Amen.

NO MORE GRUDGES

Be gentle and ready to forgive; never hold grudges. Remember, the Lord forgave you, so you must forgive others. Most of all, let love guide your life.

COLOSSIANS 3:13–14 TLB

Do you know what a grudge is? It is choosing to stay mad at someone because something they said or did made you upset. We all get mad sometimes, and that's OK. But God wants us to be willing to forgive others instead of staying mad at them. He knows that holding grudges only makes us unhappy. God loves us, so He chooses to forgive us. And that's how He wants us to treat others too—it helps everyone feel better (including you!). So the next time you are tempted to hold a grudge, forgive instead. You'll be glad you did!

THOUGHT OF THE DAY

Forgiving is God's way of living!

PRAY TODAY

Dear God, thank You so much for always forgiving me. Help me to let go of grudges and forgive others too! Amen.

DAY 28

GOD'S GOOD RULES

Now, Israel, listen to the laws and commands I will teach you. Obey them so that you will live.

DEUTERONOMY 4:1 NCV

What if there were no stop lights, no street signs, and no crosswalks? What if everyone just went as fast as they wanted and didn't look out for anyone else? Walking and driving around would be very dangerous! People make good rules so everyone stays safe. That's what God does too. He gives us good rules in the Bible like "love one another," "tell the truth," "be kind," and "don't hurt each other." When we follow God's rules, everyone stays safe. Obeying God's good rules is the best way to live.

THOUGHT OF THE DAY

Good rules help us live good lives.

PRAY TODAY

Dear God, I'm glad You gave us good rules. Please help me to follow them each day! Amen.

GOD'S GIFTS

For the LORD God is our sun and our shield. He gives us grace and glory. The LORD will withhold no good thing from those who do what is right.

PSALM 84:11 NLT

Isn't it exciting to get gifts at Christmas and on your birthday? Your friends and family give you gifts because they love you and want you to be happy. But do you know who else loves to give you gifts? God! God gives you sunshine and rain, a body that is growing, friends and family who care about you, and the ability to learn new things. God's gifts don't cost money, but they are more precious than anything you could buy. God gives you gifts because He loves you more than you can imagine.

THOUGHT OF THE DAY

Can you name some of the wonderful gifts God has given you?

PRAY TODAY

Dear God, thank You for giving me so much. Please help me use the gifts You have given me to bless others. Amen.

DAY 30

BE KIND AND FORGIVE

Be kind and compassionate to one another, forgiving each other, just as in Christ God forgave you.

EPHESIANS 4:32 NIV

When someone breaks your toy or hurts your feelings, you probably feel sad or mad. You might even want to get even by breaking something of theirs or saying something hurtful back to them. But that just makes the hurt go on and on. Jesus shows us a better way. He reminds us that He always forgives us. We can copy Jesus by being kind and caring towards others too. We can forgive them. We can refuse to get even or hurt others back. When we forgive, we are showing love, and that makes God happy!

THOUGHT OF THE DAY

The best way to live is to be kind and forgive!

PRAY TODAY

Dear Jesus, thank You for forgiving me when I make mistakes. Please help me to be kind and forgiving toward others. Amen.

DAY 31

THE PERFECT PRESENT

God loves the person who gives happily.

2 CORINTHIANS 9:7B ICB

It's fun to pick out just the right gift for someone you love! You can wrap it in pretty paper and look forward to the moment they'll open it.

But sometimes giving isn't so fun. It's hard to give your time to a sibling who needs help, or to put some of your allowance in the offering plate, or to give a friend your last cookie. But God says that each time we give something away, we should do it cheerfully. So next time you have a chance to share what you have, imagine you're wrapping up a beautiful birthday present. Then hand it over with a smile!

THOUGHT OF THE DAY

Being a cheerful giver takes practice. Look for ways to share what you have each day!

PRAY TODAY

Dear God, please help me share with a smile. It's hard to give things away sometimes, and I could use Your help. Amen.

DAY 32

WAYS TO PRAISE

The LORD is my strength and song; He has become my salvation. This is my God, and I will praise Him.

EXODUS 15:2 HCSB

The best gift you can give God is your praise. He loves to see you enjoy His world, and to hear what makes you happy. You probably know you can praise God when you pray. But did you know you can use your special gifts to praise Him in SO many other ways too?

You can make up a song to say what you're thankful for, or create a joyful dance just for Him! Try drawing a picture of something you love. Even asking questions and learning more about the world shows God how much you appreciate His creation. How will you choose to praise God today?

THOUGHT OF THE DAY

Praise God any kind of way. Try to do it every day!

PRAY TODAY

Dear God, You are amazing! I love You and I want to praise You any way I can! Amen.

YOU'RE IMPORTANT TO GOD

God began doing a good work in you, and I am sure he will continue it until it is finished when Jesus Christ comes again.

PHILIPPIANS 1:6 NCV

God has great plans for you. And those plans have already started! God can use everything you learn and experience to help develop your gifts. He brings people into your life who will encourage and support you. He's listening every time you pray, guiding you to make good choices and to learn from your mistakes. He is with you every moment of every day.

Sometimes it feels like nothing goes right. But when that happens, try to remember God's great love. He's doing good work in you, and He'll keep doing it. You are so important to Him!

THOUGHT OF THE DAY

You're a big part of God's plan!

PRAY TODAY

Dear God, it feels good to know I matter so much to You! Thanks for doing good work in me. Amen.

DAY 34

PEACE STARTS AT HOME

How wonderful, how beautiful, when brothers and sisters get along!

PSALM 133:1 MSG

Families are a gift from God. But it's normal to argue sometimes. What's important is how you work through your disagreements. Next time you feel an argument starting, try the "3 Fs."

Be Friendly: Choose kind words instead of mean ones.

Be Flexible: Look for a solution that works for everyone—not just you.

Be Forgiving: Remember that everyone makes mistakes. Can you be the one who offers forgiveness first?

You won't always agree with everyone in your family. But when you work hard to get along, your home will be loving and peaceful!

THOUGHT OF THE DAY

You can use the 3 Fs with friends and classmates too!

PRAY TODAY

Dear God, help me get along with my family, even when we disagree. I love having a peaceful home! Amen.

CONTINUE SEEKING GOD

"Continue to ask, and God will give to you. Continue to search, and you will find. Continue to knock, and the door will open for you."

MATTHEW 7:7 ICB

When you are just learning something new, it's easy to get discouraged. Whether you are learning how to sound out words, how to kick a ball, or how to sing a song, it will take many tries to get it right or do it well. But if you don't continue, you may not learn at all! Learning about God also takes practice. When you practice praying, it becomes easier. When you practice trusting God, your faith grows. When you practice doing what God says, you become a stronger believer. Continue seeking God and He promises you will find Him!

THOUGHT OF THE DAY

How will you seek God today?

PRAY TODAY

Dear God, I'm glad You want me to find You. Please help me seek You each day. Amen.

LIVING IN UNITY

How good and how pleasant it is when God's people live together in unity!

PSALM 133:1 NIV

Have you noticed how everyone is different? Some of us are tall and some are short. We have different colored hair and skin. Some of us love sports while others love art or reading. Some like to be loud, and others prefer quiet. Some of us live in cities and some live in the country. Even with all these differences, God wants us to live together in unity. Unity means that we care about each other and try hard to understand and learn from one another. When we live in unity, God says it is good for everyone!

THOUGHT OF THE DAY

How are you the same as, and different from, your friends?

PRAY TODAY

Dear God, thank You for our differences. Help me to treat each person I know with the same love You show me. Amen.

BE CONSIDERATE

Let everyone see that you are considerate in all you do.

PHILIPPIANS 4:5A NLT

Do you know what it means to be considerate? It means to consider—or think about—others' feelings. If you notice that someone has been left out, you might talk to them and invite them to play with you. If a friend isn't sure how to solve a problem, you could help them think of solutions. If others make fun of someone, you can choose kindness by standing up for them instead. Being considerate means treating others the way you would like to be treated. It's that simple!

THOUGHT OF THE DAY

How can you be considerate at home today?

PRAY TODAY

Dear God, thank You for loving and caring about me. Please help me to be more considerate of others. Amen.

NEVER ALONE

"Be sure of this—that I am with you always, even to the end of the world."

MATTHEW 28:20B TLB

Just before He returned to heaven, Jesus made a promise to His friends. He said, "I am with you always." It's a promise for you too! When you are feeling alone or lonely, you can remember that Jesus is always with you. An easy way to remember this is to hold up one of your hands, then touch each of your fingers with your other hand. As you touch each finger, say the five words in this verse: I—am—with—you—always. Then put your hand over your heart to remind you that Jesus is there.

THOUGHT OF THE DAY

You are never alone because Jesus is always with you.

PRAY TODAY

Thank You, Jesus, for loving me and always being with me. Amen.

BEING AFRAID

"Don't be afraid, for I am with you. Don't be discouraged, for I am your God. I will strengthen you and help you. I will hold you up with my victorious right hand."

ISAIAH 41:10 NLT

God knows that everyone gets afraid sometimes. Even grown-ups feel afraid! When a friend or family member is nearby and holds our hand, it helps calm our fear. Knowing that someone is with us makes us less afraid because we know we're not alone. But sometimes, there's no one nearby to hold our hand. That's when it is great to know that God says "I will hold you up with my victorious right hand." When you're afraid, God is always right there with you. Trust Him to hold you and help you be brave.

THOUGHT OF THE DAY

When you fear, remember God is near!

PRAY TODAY

Thank You, God, for understanding that sometimes I'm afraid. Help me remember that You are always with me. Amen.

DAY 40

BE A GIVER

"Give, and you will receive. Your gift will return to you in full—pressed down, shaken together to make room for more, running over, and poured into your lap. The amount you give will determine the amount you get back."

LUKE 6:38 NLT

How do you feel when someone gives you something or shares with you? Doesn't it make you want to share with them too? Good friends know that being a giver not only makes others happy, it makes them happy too! How can you be a giver? You can help someone learn something. You can share a snack or toy. You can draw a picture for someone. You can give them your attention and listen well. When you're a giver, others will also give to you! It makes every day more fun.

THOUGHT OF THE DAY

What are some ways you can be a giver today?

PRAY TODAY

Dear God, thank You for giving me so many blessings. Help me be a giver too. Amen.

SURPRISE THEM!

Don't repay evil for evil. Don't retaliate with insults when people insult you. Instead, pay them back with a blessing.

1 PETER 3:9A NLT

When someone is kind to you, it's easy to be kind in return. But what about when someone says something mean, or does something you don't like? Should you be mean back?

No! In fact, God says you should surprise them with kindness! If they use hurtful words, find helpful words to say. If someone takes something away from you, don't take something in return. And remember to pray for them later! When you choose gentleness instead of anger, God will bless you with peace and joy. And maybe even a new friend! What a great surprise!

THOUGHT OF THE DAY

Maybe someone just needs help being kind. You can lead the way!

PRAY TODAY

Dear God, please show me how to surprise others with blessings today. Amen.

YOU BRING GOD JOY

"For the LORD your God is living among you. He is a mighty savior. He will take delight in you with gladness. With his love, he will calm all your fears. He will rejoice over you with joyful songs."

ZEPHANIAH 3:17 NLT

Do you know that you make God happy? The Bible says that God takes "delight in you with gladness" and that he "will rejoice over you with joyful songs." God loves watching over you and knowing what you're doing. He is excited when you learn new things and your accomplishments bring Him joy. Because He is a loving Father, God celebrates when you do well. So whenever you are feeling small or unimportant, just remember that you are special and you bring great joy to God, your Savior!

THOUGHT OF THE DAY

You make God happy just by being YOU!

PRAY TODAY

Thank You, God, for loving me so much. I'm so glad that I can bring You joy! Amen.

DAY 43

HELP YOUR FAMILY

The one who lives with integrity is righteous; his children who come after him will be happy.

PROVERBS 20:7 HCSB

Today's Bible verse says that when families live with "integrity," they are happy. Integrity means to be honest, to think of others first, and to do what is right. You can help your family to be happy by learning to making thoughtful choices. When you do something wrong, be honest and tell the truth. When you promise to do something for your parents, be sure you do it. Choose kindness! You will help your family be happy when you live with integrity!

THOUGHT OF THE DAY

How will you show integrity today?

PRAY TODAY

Dear God, thank You for giving me a family. Please help me to live with integrity, so I can help us all be happy! Amen.

DAY 44

WHAT ARE YOU DOING?

Here's what you do: Live well, live wisely, live humbly. It's the way you live, not the way you talk, that counts.

JAMES 3:13B MSG

Have you ever heard the expression, "Actions speak louder than words"? What that means is that what we do tells people more about us than what we say. If you say you play fair, but then you cheat at a game, what do your actions say about you? If you make a promise, but then you break it, will people believe what you say?

Our words are important, but our actions are even more important. Show everyone the kind of person you are by doing what is right and treating others with kindness. That's the wise way to live.

THOUGHT OF THE DAY

Let your actions show others that you belong to Jesus.

PRAY TODAY

Dear God, I want to please You by what I do and say. Please help me to show others that I am Your child. Amen.

CHOOSE GOD'S WAY

"Choose this day whom you will serve. . . . But as for me and my house, we will serve the LORD."

JOSHUA 24:15 ESV

Do you know what it means to be free? When you are free, you are able to make choices. Since you're still young, your parents probably help you make good choices each day. But there are lots of decisions you can still make for yourself!

Your choices make a big difference in how your day will go. Will you choose to be kind or be mean? Will you choose to share or be selfish? Will you choose to obey the rules or break the rules? When you have to make a choice, stop and think about what the Lord would have you do. Then choose His way. It is always good.

THOUGHT OF THE DAY

Lots of choices, big and small. Let God help you with them all!

PRAY TODAY

Dear God, thank You for giving me the freedom to make choices. Please help me to choose to do things Your way. Amen.

STRONG HEARTS

Those with pure hearts shall become stronger and stronger.

JOB 17:9B TLB

If you want to have strong muscles, you can practice running and do exercises. But how do you get a stronger heart? The Bible says that we can get strong hearts by practicing pure things.

Pure things are actions that help you follow God. You can learn Scripture verses, sing songs of praise, and watch and read stories that teach you how to be more like Jesus. When you spend your time doing things like that, your heart gets stronger. And with a strong heart, it's easier to do things God's way!

THOUGHT OF THE DAY

What's something you are doing to make your heart strong and pure?

PRAY TODAY

Dear God, please help me to follow You, so that my heart can grow strong and pure. Amen.

DAY 47

LOVE AND HONOR

Love each other with genuine affection, and take delight in honoring each other.

ROMANS 12:10 NLT

One of the best ways to make good friends is to be a good friend! But do you know how to do that?

God gives us some clues! First, love your friends. When you love people, you treat them kindly and help when they're having a hard time. Then, He asks us to honor our friends. Have you ever cheered for a friend who's playing a soccer game or performing in the talent show? Those are both great ways to honor your friends. And when you love and honor others, chances are they will love and honor you too!

THOUGHT OF THE DAY

Honoring friends should be fun! What's a creative way to celebrate someone today?

PRAY TODAY

Dear God, thank You for good friends! Please show me ways to love and honor others every day! Amen.

WIN OR LOSE

Happiness comes to those who are fair to others and are always just and good.

PSALM 106:3 TLB

Do you like playing games? Who do you like to play with? It's most fun to play a game with people who follow the rules, right?

Following the rules of a game means you won't always win. And that's OK! Losing can be disappointing, but you can still have fun playing. The most important thing is to play fair. Don't try to break the rules just so you can win. That's called cheating, and it's no fun for anyone else. Instead, try your best, and say "Hooray!" for whoever wins! Everyone loves to play with someone who plays fair and has fun.

THOUGHT OF THE DAY

What's your favorite game?

PRAY TODAY

Dear God, sometimes it's so hard to lose. Please help me feel peaceful and calm, no matter who wins. Amen.

DAY 49

GOD BLESSED YOU

Every good gift and every perfect gift is from above, coming down from the Father of lights.

JAMES 1:17 ESV

Are you interested in something unique? Maybe you feel out of place, because no one seems to be just like you. Or maybe you feel like there's nothing very special about you at all! Here's the truth: God has blessed you with good gifts He chose just for you. And He wants you to use them! Your gifts could be talents, like singing or playing sports. Your gifts could be attributes, like being kind, generous, or wise. Maybe you're a great leader or an excellent listener. Ask God to show you the gifts He's given you. Then practice using them every day!

THOUGHT OF THE DAY

Every gift God gives is good. Are you using yours? You should!

PRAY TODAY

Dear God, please help me see my gifts, and show me how to use them! Amen.

DAY 50

UNCHANGING LOVE

"I have loved you with a love that lasts forever. I have kept on loving you with a kindness that never fails."

JEREMIAH 31:3B NIRV

Lots of things change. Have you ever had a special toy that wore out or broke? Maybe you had a friend who moved away. And if you look back at pictures of yourself when you were a baby, you will see how much you have changed! People and things don't stay the same. But do you know what never changes? God's love for you!

In the Bible God says that His love lasts forever and His kindness never fails. You can always count on God, no matter what happens. He will never wear out, move away, or change.

THOUGHT OF THE DAY

Count on God's love because it's true. His kindness is always there for you.

PRAY TODAY

Dear God, thank You for always loving me, for never changing, and for always being kind. Amen.

DAY 51

SMILES BRING HAPPINESS

Smiling faces make you happy, and good news makes you feel better.

PROVERBS 15:30 GNT

Some scientists did an interesting experiment. They asked people to smile, even if they weren't feeling happy. Do you know what happened? The people who put a smile on their faces soon started to feel happier! But this isn't a new discovery. Thousands of years ago, King Solomon wrote in the Bible that "smiling faces make you happy"! He also said, "good news makes you feel better." So the next time you want to feel happy, try putting a smile on your face. And then share some good news with someone. Chances are you will feel better soon, and so will they!

THOUGHT OF THE DAY

When you put a smile on your face, happy feelings follow!

PRAY TODAY

Dear God, thank You for helping me to smile and feel happy. Please help me share good news with others too! Amen.

DAY 52

GOD COMES FIRST

"Do not have other gods besides Me."

EXODUS 20:3 HCSB

God gave us a list of good rules called the Ten Commandments. Some rules tell us how to live with others, but the first three are all about how we should live with God. That's because God should always come first in our life. We should love Him with our whole heart, and nothing should ever become more important than God. And when we use God's name, we should always talk about Him with love and respect. Those rules are listed before the others because when we love God first, loving others is easy!

THOUGHT OF THE DAY

Put God first each day—say a prayer as soon as you wake up!

PRAY TODAY

Dear God, sometimes I forget that You are most important. Help me put You first and love You well. Amen.

DAY 53

COURAGE TO WAIT

Wait for the Lord; be strong, and let your heart take courage; wait for the Lord!

PSALM 27:14 ESV

When you think of courage you might think of doing something really exciting! But sometimes the bravest thing you can do is trust God and wait for Him to work.

God promised the great Bible hero Joshua that he would capture the town of Jericho. But Joshua had to spend seven days just walking around the town. It must have been hard to wait! But Joshua trusted that God would fulfill His promise, and on the seventh day, He did! Next time you're having a hard time waiting for something to happen, remember Joshua. Trust God to do big things at just the right time!

THOUGHT OF THE DAY

What's something you're waiting for?

PRAY TODAY

Dear God, it's hard to wait! Please give me courage to trust You. Amen.

DAY 54

LOVE YOUR NEIGHBOR

If you really keep the royal law according to the Scripture, "Love your neighbor as yourself," you are doing right.

JAMES 2:8 NIV

The Bible says that if you love your neighbor, you're doing a great job. But does that mean you should just love the people in your neighborhood? Nope! According to God, a neighbor can be anyone! Is a classmate feeling lonely? Sit next to him at lunch. Is your sister frustrated learning something new? Help or encourage her! Even people in other parts of the world are your neighbors! You can help them by praying for them or supporting missionaries who bring God's Word to faraway places. Loving your neighbor is important work!

THOUGHT OF THE DAY

Who is a "neighbor" you can love today?

PRAY TODAY

Dear God, thank You for all my neighbors! Help me love each one I meet today. Amen.

YOU AND GOD CAN DO IT!

As Goliath moved closer to attack, David quickly ran out to meet him.

1 SAMUEL 17:48 NLT

In the story of David and Goliath, David isn't the kind of hero you'd expect. He's not a trained soldier. In fact, he's only at the battlefield to bring food to his brothers. But when no one else will fight the scary giant Goliath, David volunteers. He trusts that God will help him, and runs right out to face Goliath. And he wins!

Is there something you need to do that's making you nervous? God can help! He made you to do exciting, brave, and important things. So pray and ask for His help. When you trust in Him, you can do anything!

THOUGHT OF THE DAY

When you feel nervous, just recall that God can help you do it all!

PRAY TODAY

Dear God, thank You for helping me do great things! Help me trust You whenever I feel afraid. Amen.

DAY 56

LIGHTEN YOUR LOAD

Worry is a heavy burden, but a kind word always brings cheer.

PROVERBS 12:25 CEV

God wants us to be happy in His world. He's given us good friends and families, and special talents. But we can't enjoy all He's done if we're stuck with a bunch of worries.

When you're worried all the time, it's like dragging around a giant suitcase. You get tired and grouchy, and you can't go very far! God wants to take all your worries away so you can live the life He's planned for you. So next time you start worrying, imagine handing your suitcase to God. Then find something you can thank Him for!

THOUGHT OF THE DAY

The Bible says a kind word can bring cheer. Try sharing kind words with yourself!

PRAY TODAY

Dear God, I don't like carrying around heavy worries. Please take my worries away so I can enjoy You more. Amen.

HEALING A DIVIDED HOUSE

"If a kingdom is divided against itself, that kingdom cannot stand. If a house is divided against itself, that house cannot stand."

MARK 3:24–25 NIV

Families can be lots of fun when we work and play together, help one another, and share with each other. But sometimes family members get angry with one another, disagree, or say unkind words. The Bible calls this a "divided house." When a house is divided, no one is happy.

When we take time to listen to one another and try to understand each other, a divided house can be put back together. Forgiving, loving, helping, being kind, and sharing are all ways to keep a house from becoming divided. When we all work together, we can heal a divided house.

THOUGHT OF THE DAY

What are some things you do to help your home be a happy one?

PRAY TODAY

Dear God, thank You for my family. Help us love each other well. Amen.

GOD GIVES WISDOM

If any of you lacks wisdom, you should ask God, who gives generously to all without finding fault, and it will be given to you.

JAMES 1:5 NIV

Sometimes the Veggies get stuck. Maybe Larry and Bob are arguing. Or Junior doesn't know how to make a new friend. Or Petunia can't solve a tricky problem.

Do you ever feel that way? It takes wisdom to figure out hard things! Fortunately, God is always wise. And the Bible promises that if you ask God, He will give wisdom to you! You don't have to be smart enough to solve all your problems. You just need to be smart enough to ask God to help you!

THOUGHT OF THE DAY

God's wisdom is always good and true. Just ask! He'll give it freely to you.

PRAY TODAY

Dear God, I am so glad You promise to give me wisdom. Please help me remember to ask You when I don't know what to do. Amen.

DAY 59

GOD'S PERFECT LOVE

No one has ever seen God; if we love one another, God abides in us and his love is perfected in us.

1 JOHN 4:12 ESV

Do you know anyone who never does anything wrong? Of course not! The Bible says no one is perfect except for God. But we CAN be part of God's perfection!

When you love others, God's love is made perfect in you. That means God's love grows bigger inside you—which means more for you and more to share! It also means your love will start to look like God's. Using helpful words, showing patience, listening to others' ideas, and welcoming new friends are all ways you can show God's love. You don't have to be perfect. But God's love can be perfected in you!

THOUGHT OF THE DAY

What are some ways you can show God's love today?

PRAY TODAY

Dear God, I am so glad that You are perfect. Please make Your love perfect in me each day. Amen.

DAY 60

KIND THOUGHTS

A wise person is patient. He will be honored if he ignores a wrong done against him.

PROVERBS 19:11 ICB

God tells us to forgive each other. That means we don't repay meanness with meanness. But it also means changing the way we think about the person who hurt us.

It's easy to think kind thoughts about people who make us happy. But what about when someone makes you angry or sad? God still wants you to think kindly about them. Don't sit around and feel angry. Instead, pray for them. You can even ask God to bless them. Remember that everyone makes mistakes. When you stop being angry and start thinking kind thoughts again, that's true forgiveness!

THOUGHT OF THE DAY

Forgiveness takes patience and practice. Keep asking God for help!

PRAY TODAY

Dear God, forgiveness can be hard. Please help me think only kind thoughts. Amen.

GOD, THE GREAT TEACHER

If you don't know what you're doing, pray to the Father. He loves to help.

JAMES 1:5 MSG

If you want to get better at something, it helps to have a great teacher. God wants you to grow in wisdom—and He's the best teacher there is!

What does it mean to grow in wisdom? It means you are always looking for ways to make God happy. It means you make friends with people who are different from you, because God loves everyone. It means you find ways to be kind and caring. And if you don't know what to do, it means your first step is talking to God. He'll teach you everything you need to know!

THOUGHT OF THE DAY

Are you not sure which way to go? Pray, and God will let you know!

PRAY TODAY

Dear God, thank You for being the best teacher! Please help me grow in wisdom every day. Amen.

DAY 62

THE GIFT OF RESPECT

Being respected is more important than having great riches.

PROVERBS 22:1 ICB

Do you know that you have something you can give to others that is more valuable than money or jewels? It's called "respect." Here are five different ways you can give respect to others:

1. Listen to what they say. Everyone likes to be heard.
2. Tell them why you like them. Give honest compliments.
3. Serve them. Look for ways to help.
4. Be kind. Take turns and use helpful words.
5. Be polite. Say please and thank you!

When we give respect to others, we are giving them a wonderful gift—and building good friendships too!

THOUGHT OF THE DAY

Choose one way to give respect to someone you know today.

PRAY TODAY

Dear God, please show me how to give respect to others today. Thank You for helping me be a good friend. Amen.

THE BEST THINGS

Don't be obsessed with getting more material things. Be relaxed with what you have.

HEBREWS 13:5 MSG

Do you ever want more stuff? Maybe a friend has a toy that you wish you had. It's normal to want things. But when wanting becomes all you think about, that's called jealousy. And jealousy doesn't feel good.

God wants you to think about what you do have instead of what you don't have, like the toys you love to play with or your favorite bedtime book. But most important, think about everyone who loves you—including God! Family, friends, and God's love are the very best things you can ever have.

THOUGHT OF THE DAY

When you start to feel jealous, try naming three things you already have that make you happy!

PRAY TODAY

Dear God, You have given me really good gifts. Help me remember them instead of wanting what someone else has! Amen.

DAY 64

MAKE FEAR DISAPPEAR

There is no fear in love, but perfect love casts out fear.

1 JOHN 4:18 ESV

Did you know that God is love? When God is with you, you have love inside you. The Bible tells us that "perfect love casts out fear." That means that when we are filled with God's love, there's no room left for fear.

The next time you feel afraid, think about God's love for you. Remember that He is always with you and that He is greater and more powerful than any of your fears. As you think more about God's great love, your fears will get smaller and smaller. And soon, they will be gone!

THOUGHT OF THE DAY

God's great love makes fear disappear!

PRAY TODAY

Dear God, thank You for Your perfect love that is more powerful than my fears. Amen.

HARD TIMES

"If you'll hold on to me for dear life," says God, "I'll get you out of any trouble. I'll give you the best of care if you'll only get to know and trust me. Call me and I'll answer, be at your side in bad times."

PSALM 91:14–15A MSG

Have you ever had a really hard day? Maybe things didn't go your way, or you kept getting in trouble. Maybe you felt angry or sad, and couldn't figure out how to feel better. Guess what? God is with you, even in those really hard times.

God gives us a great promise: If we stay close to Him, He can get us through anything. When you trust God, He holds your hand every day. And He's always listening when you pray. So reach out for Him! He is waiting to lead you through every day, in good times and bad.

THOUGHT OF THE DAY

God is a wonderful friend!

PRAY TODAY

Dear God, thank You for never leaving my side. Please remind me to talk to You when I have hard days. Amen.

WORDS ARE GIFTS

Say only what helps, each word a gift.

EPHESIANS 4:29B MSG

Did you know that your words can be a gift to someone? Your words can help someone who is having a hard time. They can cheer up someone who is sad. Kind words can let someone know you love them.

Maybe someone needs to hear "I care about you." Or perhaps they need to hear "How can I help?" Did you know that "I'm sorry" and "I will pray for you" are also words that show kindness? If you don't know what to say, just ask God to give you helpful words. Make your words a gift to someone today!

THOUGHT OF THE DAY

When friends or family need a lift, your helpful words can be a gift!

PRAY TODAY

Dear God, please help me use my words as gifts of kindness and love. Amen.

DAY 67

SING FOR JOY

Shout with joy to the Lord, all the earth! Worship the Lord with gladness. Come before him, singing with joy.

PSALM 100:1–2 NLT

What do you do when you are really happy? Do you jump up and down? Sing a song? Wave your arms and laugh? It's hard to keep joy inside, isn't it?

The Bible tells us about a great king named David who wrote songs, played the harp, and shouted for joy when he was happy. David knew that God loves to hear His people praise Him and sing to Him when they are happy. God created us to find joy in life, and He loves it when we share that joy with others too!

THOUGHT OF THE DAY

What are some ways you can think of to show God you are filled with joy?

PRAY TODAY

Dear God, thank You for loving me and giving me so many things to be happy about. Amen.

DAY 68

A QUIET TIME

Let all that I am wait quietly before God, for my hope is in him.

PSALM 62:5 NLT

Do you love being with friends? Because Jesus wants to be your good friend, He loves when you choose to spend time with Him too. But how do you spend time with a friend you can't see?

Some people set aside a few minutes each day for a quiet time with God. They might pray, read Bible verses, sing songs about God, or just be still and wait for God's thoughts to come to their mind. Spending time with a friend is how you get to know each other better. Spending time with God works the same way!

THOUGHT OF THE DAY

When can you spend some quiet time with Jesus today?

PRAY TODAY

Dear God, I want to know You better. Please help me find time to be quiet with You today. Amen.

CHOOSE FAITH

I have chosen the way of faithfulness; I set your rules before me.

PSALM 119:30 ESV

King David made a very good choice. He decided that he wanted to have faith in God and remember His rules. But King David wasn't perfect. Sometimes he was selfish and made up his own rules instead. Sometimes he ignored people who reminded him to follow God! But each time he made mistakes, he chose to return to God and ask forgiveness. Then he tried again. You can do that too! God doesn't expect you to get everything right. But when you ask forgiveness and keep trying, God will grow your faith. You can choose God over and over, just like King David!

THOUGHT OF THE DAY

The only way your faith will grow is choosing God wherever you go.

PRAY TODAY

Dear God, please help me remember Your rules. Thank You that I can always come back to You if I make mistakes. Amen.

COMMON COURTESY

Remind them . . . to avoid quarreling, to be gentle, and to show perfect courtesy toward all people.

TITUS 3:1A AND 2B ESV

The Bible tells us to show courtesy—or good manners—to all people. That's because each person is important to God. So remember to say thank you whenever someone helps you, whether it's your grandma, your best friend, or the server at a restaurant! Try holding the door open for the person behind you when you go into a store or your classroom. Be sure to knock before you go into your sibling's room—that shows them you respect their privacy! Good manners help you show God's love every day.

THOUGHT OF THE DAY

Don't make manners something rare. Common courtesy shows you care!

PRAY TODAY

Dear God, it's cool that I can show Your love just by being polite! Help me remember my good manners every day. Amen.

EXTRA PEACE

Now may the Lord of peace himself give you peace at all times in every way. The Lord be with you all.

2 THESSALONIANS 3:16 ESV

Peace is one of God's greatest gifts. It can help you feel calm, confident, and even hopeful when things don't go your way.

Sometimes it's hard to find peace. After all, it's normal to feel upset when you don't get what you want. So try asking God to give you an extra helping of peace at extra hard times. He never runs out, and He loves to give His children good things. And a peaceful heart is the very best thing!

THOUGHT OF THE DAY

A trusting heart is a peaceful heart.

PRAY TODAY

Dear God, thank You for the gift of peace, and thank You that I can always ask for more! Amen.

DAY 72

PRAY FOR EVERYONE

First of all, I ask you to pray for everyone. Ask God to help and bless them all, and tell God how thankful you are for each of them.

1 TIMOTHY 2:1 CEV

Talking to God is a powerful thing. So why not use that power to help others? Praying for other people is one of the best ways to care for them. If you know them well, you can pray for something you know they need. Or just give thanks for the people in your life, and ask God to bless them. You can even pray for people you've never met! God loves everyone, and we all need His help—from your best friend to the president. Prayer may seem like a small thing. But it's a super important job!

THOUGHT OF THE DAY

Make a list of five people to pray for every day. Try to include at least one person you don't know!

PRAY TODAY

Dear God, I'm so glad You love all of us. Please help me show Your love to everyone I meet today. Amen.

JESUS LOVES YOU

"As the Father has loved Me, I have also loved you. Remain in My love."

JOHN 15:9 HCSB

Do you know the song "Jesus Loves Me"? It goes: "Jesus loves me this I know, for the Bible tells me so!" It is a simple song, but it contains one of the most amazing facts you'll ever know: Jesus loves you!

That is amazing because Jesus created the whole universe and everything in it. He made stars and planets, gigantic mountains and seas, and tiny bugs and birds. And He loves you! You are very special to God. So, whenever you feel lonely or sad, remember that Jesus, who made the whole world, loves you!

THOUGHT OF THE DAY

God's Word is always right and true, so you can trust that God loves you!

PRAY TODAY

Dear God, thank You for loving me always, no matter what. Amen.

DAY 74

THE WAY TO GOD

Yes, it is through Christ we all have the right to come to the Father in one Spirit.

EPHESIANS 2:18 NCV

When you go for a drive somewhere, how does the driver know the way? They might follow a map, street signs, or listen to directions on the car's GPS. If we want to get closer to God, how can we know the way?

The Bible says that to find the way to God, we need to follow Jesus. We can follow Jesus by doing what He tells us in the Bible: be kind, love one another, pray, and forgive each other. Jesus always shows us the way to God. He never leads us in the wrong direction.

THOUGHT OF THE DAY

What's one thing you can do to follow Jesus today?

PRAY TODAY

Dear God, I want to get closer to You. Please help me to follow Jesus more today. Amen.

GOD'S SUPER-POWER

Finally, be strong in the Lord and in his mighty power.

EPHESIANS 6:10 NIV

There are lots of books and movies about superheroes with special powers. Some superheroes can fly or climb straight up walls! Sometimes it's fun to dress up in a cape and pretend to be a superhero.

But do you know who has more power than any superhero you've ever heard of? God! He created mountains and oceans and all the planets and stars. When you trust in God to help you, you are counting on His super strength and power. His strength is real and He loves to use His power to help you!

THOUGHT OF THE DAY

How would you like God to help you today?

PRAY TODAY

Dear God, thank You for being so powerful. Help me depend on Your strength today. Amen.

DAY 76

FAITH THAT GROWS

Immediately the father of the child cried out and said with tears, "Lord, I believe; help my unbelief!"

MARK 9:24 NKJV

The Bible tells a story about a father who brought his sick son to Jesus. Jesus told the man that He would heal the boy. But the father was afraid that he didn't have enough faith in Jesus, so he asked Jesus to help him believe even more. Then Jesus prayed over the boy and made him well.

Sometimes it is hard to believe that Jesus can help us, but, just like the father in the story, we can always pray for more faith. Jesus wants us to trust in Him and, if we ask, He will always help our faith grow.

THOUGHT OF THE DAY

Faith is like a flower that grows when we water it with prayer.

PRAY TODAY

Dear God, please help me to trust and believe in You more and more every day. Amen.

DAY 77

JESUS' TEAM

"This is how everyone will recognize that you are my disciples—when they see the love you have for each other."

JOHN 13:35 MSG

When you join a sports team, you usually get a uniform. When you wear it, everyone knows you belong to that team. But how do we tell people that we belong to Jesus? He doesn't give us a special uniform. Instead, Jesus said that everyone will know we are on His team if we show love to others. You can tell everyone you're on Jesus' team by being kind and helpful. You can forgive others when they make mistakes and help someone who is hurting or sad. Love is the "uniform" of Jesus' followers. Be sure to wear it every day!

THOUGHT OF THE DAY

How will you show you're on Jesus' team today?

PRAY TODAY

Dear God, I love being on Your team! Please help me remember to wear my uniform of love every day. Amen.

HOW TO LEARN

Remember what you are taught. And listen carefully to words of knowledge.

PROVERBS 23:12 ICB

Have you ever played sports or taken dance or music lessons? What if your coach or teacher tells you how to do something, but you ignore them? You won't be a very good teammate, and chances are you'll never learn to dance or play music either!

If we want to improve at something, we need to listen to our parents, coaches, and teachers. And then we need to remember and practice what they teach us. God sends good teachers to help us. When we do as they say, we learn and get better!

THOUGHT OF THE DAY

What is something you are learning? What are you doing to get better at it?

PRAY TODAY

Dear God, thank You for giving me good teachers. Please help me listen, practice, and learn well. Amen.

FILL YOUR HOME WITH LOVE

But Ruth said, "Don't beg me to leave you or to stop following you. Where you go, I will go. Where you live, I will live. Your people will be my people, and your God will be my God."

RUTH 1:16 NCV

Ruth was a woman who loved her family. She worked hard and made good choices that helped keep her family safe and healthy. And even when she faced hard times, she chose to help, be kind, and show love. Ruth knew that family is a special gift from God.

Strong, happy families have lots of love and kindness. It's normal to get frustrated or annoyed sometimes, especially with the people you see every day! But try to find ways to fill your home with love whenever you can. That's the way to make your family feel joyful, safe, and fun!

THOUGHT OF THE DAY

How does your family show love for each other?

PRAY TODAY

Dear God, thank You for my family! Help us to show love to each other every day. Amen.

GROWING AND CHANGING

There is a time for everything, and a season for every activity under the heavens.

ECCLESIASTES 3:1 NIV

Sometimes Junior Asparagus wishes everything could stay the same. He likes what he's doing, he likes where he lives, and he likes how old he is! But have you noticed that everything in the world changes? The sun comes up and it goes down, the seasons change, it's lovely one day and stormy the next. You are changing too. You're getting taller, you're learning to do more things, your family needs you to help out more. Change is sometimes hard, but it is also good. It means you are growing. You are becoming the person God created you to be!

THOUGHT OF THE DAY

What are some ways you have changed since your last birthday?

PRAY TODAY

Dear God, thank You for helping me grow. Please help me become the person You want me to be. Amen.

A CHEERFUL HEART

A cheerful heart is good medicine, but a broken spirit saps a person's strength.

PROVERBS 17:22 NLT

You may not be a doctor or a nurse, but you can still help a sick friend feel better. How? You can draw a picture for them, send them a card, connect with them on the phone or computer, or pray for God to help them get well. These are all ways to spread some cheer—and the Bible says that "a cheerful heart is good medicine"! And even if their body is OK, a friend might feel sad or lonely. Your cheerful heart can help them feel better too!

THOUGHT OF THE DAY

What is one way you can cheer up someone today?

PRAY TODAY

Dear God, please show me ways I can help others feel better by having a cheerful heart. Amen.

DAY 82

GOD LOVES YOUR LAUGH

"He will yet fill your mouth with laughter and your lips with shouts of joy."

JOB 8:21 NIV

The Veggies love to laugh. They make up silly songs and sing them to their friends. They have goofy adventures and share goofy jokes. Did you know that the Bible says God loves for His children to be happy, to laugh, and to be joyful? God has filled the world with things that bring us joy—trees with leaves that dance in the wind, puppies that wrestle and run, kittens that pounce and play. What kinds of things make you laugh? Don't be afraid to giggle, be silly, or sing for joy. God loves to hear you laugh.

THOUGHT OF THE DAY

Do something today that makes you laugh!

PRAY TODAY

Thank You, God, for caring about me and wanting me to laugh and be joyful. Amen.

DOING IS IMPORTANT

But be doers of the word and not hearers only.

JAMES 1:22A HCSB

What if you read the words in a cookbook, but you never cooked anything? What if you got a toy for your birthday, but you just looked at the directions and never put it together? It's important to do what the words say!

In the same way, we should do something about what the Bible says. When Jesus says to "love your neighbor," we need to find ways to show love. When we hear a story that reminds us to forgive, we should learn to forgive others. Hearing is just one part of God's plan. Doing is important too!

THOUGHT OF THE DAY

What is one way you will do what the Bible says today?

PRAY TODAY

Dear God, thank You for the Bible. Please help me to not just listen to the words in it, but to do what it says. Amen.

DAY 84

CLEAN AGAIN

If we tell Him our sins, He is faithful and we can depend on Him to forgive us of our sins. He will make our lives clean from all sin.

1 JOHN 1:9 NLV

When you make a mistake drawing or writing with a pencil, you can use an eraser to erase the mistake and start over. When you get dirt on your clothes, you can wash them and make them clean again. But what happens if you do something wrong, or hurt someone with your words or actions? God says that if we tell Him about the wrong things we do and ask Him to forgive us, He will! He promises to make our lives clean again, so we can start over and do better the next time.

THOUGHT OF THE DAY

Soap can clean your hands, but only God can clean your heart!

PRAY TODAY

Dear God, thank You for loving me so much. Please help me to always come to You for forgiveness. Amen.

BE GOD'S HANDS

Never walk away from someone who deserves help; your hand is God's hand for that person.

PROVERBS 3:27 MSG

Have you ever thought about how very special your hands are? You can draw with them, build with them, even use sign language to "talk" with them. But there is something even more special you can do with your hands—the Bible says you can be God's hands. How? When you help someone, when you comfort someone, when you pat someone on the back to encourage them, when you make a gift to let someone know you love them, you are showing them that God loves them too—you are being God's hands!

THOUGHT OF THE DAY

How can you be God's hands today?

PRAY TODAY

Dear God, please help me use my hands to show others that You love them. Amen.

DAY 86

ALWAYS THERE

"Do not be afraid or discouraged. For the Lord your God is with you wherever you go."

JOSHUA 1:9 NLT

Have you ever felt like you were all alone? Maybe you weren't sure what to do and felt scared, or you were discouraged because you made a mistake. God understands. He knows how you feel whether you are happy or sad, excited or worried, feeling brave or feeling afraid. And God is always right where you are, no matter where you go. You never have to feel embarrassed to share how you feel or ask Him for help. He cares for you, and He wants you to know that He will never leave you.

THOUGHT OF THE DAY

God is always there, and He will always care.

PRAY TODAY

Thank You, God, for understanding how I feel. I'm so glad You are always with me. Amen.

GOD WORKS FOR YOUR GOOD

And we know that for those who love God all things work together for good, for those who are called according to his purpose.

ROMANS 8:28 ESV

Have you ever made a mistake? Maybe you tried to kick a soccer ball, but you slipped and fell. Maybe you painted a picture, but then paint dripped on your paper. God knows that we all make mistakes. But God is so amazing, that He can take our mistakes and turn them into something good. The next time you make a mistake, ask God to make something good come out of it. Maybe you will learn how to do it better next time, or maybe your mistake will become a happy discovery of a new way to do something!

THOUGHT OF THE DAY

What will you do the next time you make a mistake?

PRAY TODAY

Dear God, I'm so glad that You can make good things come from my mistakes. Thanks for always helping me. Amen.

FOLLOWING JESUS' STEPS

For God called you to do good, even if it means suffering, just as Christ suffered for you. He is your example, and you must follow in his steps.

1 PETER 2:21 NLT

Have you ever walked behind someone in the snow or followed someone on a sandy beach? It's easy to do because you can see their footprints in the snow or sand. You can step just where they stepped!

The Bible says we should follow in Jesus' steps. But how do we do this when He lived so long ago? When you learn about Jesus and how He treated people, it's like seeing His steps. He was kind. He was forgiving. He helped others. When you do what Jesus did, you are following in His steps, and that makes God happy!

THOUGHT OF THE DAY

What is one good way you can follow in Jesus' steps today?

PRAY TODAY

Dear God, thank You for giving me the example of Jesus in the Bible. Please help me to follow in His steps today. Amen.

CELEBRATE GOD!

Celebrate God all day, every day.

PHILIPPIANS 4:4 MSG

What are your favorite celebrations? Do you love Christmas? How about Easter? Is your birthday one of your favorite days? These are special times that you usually only celebrate on one day of the year. But the Bible says we should celebrate God all day, every day!!

God blesses the earth with sunshine and rain so things can grow. He created the moon, planets, and stars to shine in the night sky. He has given you a family and friends who love you. There are so many reasons to celebrate God. Enjoy doing it every day!

THOUGHT OF THE DAY

What is one way you plan to celebrate God today?

PRAY TODAY

Dear God, thank You for being such a loving Father. I want to celebrate You today and every day. Amen.

HELPFUL BODIES

Because you were bought by God for a price. So honor God with your bodies.

1 CORINTHIANS 6:20 NCV

God created your body with many amazing parts, but He lets you choose how to use them. Your feet can run and skip, but they could hurt someone if you use them to kick. Your arms can hug, but they can also scare someone if you decide to push and shove. Your mouth can speak kind words, but it can also make someone sad if you call them names or make fun of them.

God created our bodies and He wants us to use them to do what is good and helpful. You can choose every day to honor God with your body!

THOUGHT OF THE DAY

What are some helpful ways you can use your feet, arms, and mouth?

PRAY TODAY

Dear God, thank You for my body. Please help me to use every part to honor You! Amen.

YOU'RE SPECIAL TO JESUS

"What man among you, who has 100 sheep and loses one of them, does not leave the 99 in the open field and go after the lost one until he finds it?"

LUKE 15:4 HCSB

Jesus wanted to teach His followers how special they were to Him, so He told them a story about a shepherd who had lost one of his sheep. The shepherd loved that one sheep so much that he searched everywhere for it. When he finally found it, he rejoiced and carried it safely home.

Through this story, Jesus showed us that He is like this good shepherd. Even though He has many followers, He knows and loves every single one of us. He will always care for you. How great to know that you are so very special to Jesus!

THOUGHT OF THE DAY

What will you do today to show Jesus that you love Him too?

PRAY TODAY

Dear God, thank You for knowing me and loving me. I'm so glad I'm special to You. Amen.

DAY 92

HOW TO LOVE GOD

This is love for God: to keep his commands.

1 JOHN 5:3 NIV

The Bible tells us that there's a simple way to show God you love Him: obey Him. But those simple directions aren't always easy to follow! Do you ever have a hard time obeying God? We all do sometimes. But here's some good news: God is always ready to forgive. In fact, asking for forgiveness means you're obeying one of God's commands! So keep trying to obey God. And if you make a mistake, just ask for forgiveness and try again! When you show God you want to follow His commands, He knows you love and trust Him.

THOUGHT OF THE DAY

When is it hardest to obey God? Ask Him to help you try extra hard at those moments!

PRAY TODAY

Dear God, I want to obey You. Thank You for giving me lots of chances to try again! Amen.

YOUR BEST FRIEND

"You are my friends, if you obey me. Servants don't know what their master is doing, and so I don't speak to you as my servants. I speak to you as my friends, and I have told you everything that my Father has told me."

JOHN 15:14–15 CEV

Do you have a best friend? Best friends help each other. They always stick up for one another. They care about one another and spend time together having fun. Guess what? Jesus wants to be your best friend! He will always help you and care for you. He always tells you the truth, and He never leaves you all alone. When we do what Jesus says to do, we show that Jesus is our best friend too. Isn't it great to have a best friend like Jesus?

THOUGHT OF THE DAY

Be sure to talk with Jesus every day! Talking together is how friends become *best* friends.

PRAY TODAY

Dear God, thank You for being my very best friend. I love You, and I want to be a good friend to You too! Amen.

SURPRISE!

The LORD your God is God of all gods and Lord of all lords. He is the great God, who is strong and wonderful.

DEUTERONOMY 10:17A NCV

The Bible is full of stories where God surprises people with wonderful blessings. Esther became queen even though she was never part of a royal family. The Israelites destroyed the walls of a huge city just by blasting trumpets. Mary got to be Jesus' mother!

God still loves to amaze us. When you trust God, incredible things can happen. You can make great friends in a new place. You can feel joyful even when bad things happen. God can give you ideas you'd never think of on your own. That's why it's important to pray and read your Bible each day. You never know what God might do!

THOUGHT OF THE DAY

The Bible says that God is strong and wonderful. He's also surprising!

PRAY TODAY

Dear God, I'm so glad You can do anything. I can't wait to see what You do today! Amen.

DON'T GIVE UP

Let us run with endurance the race that is set before us.

HEBREWS 12:1B ESV

If you're running a race, do you sit down before the finish line? When you're working on a model or a puzzle, do you stop halfway through?

To win a race or finish a project, you have to keep going! Life is like that too. There are many things to learn and do. Sometimes you might want to give up or quit. But the Bible tells us to keep on going, even when things are difficult or boring. After all, you'll never know the joy of finishing if you don't endure to the end!

THOUGHT OF THE DAY

When you feel like giving up, ask God to help you keep going.

PRAY TODAY

Dear God, help me remember that You are there to help me when I feel like giving up. Thank You. Amen.

RUN THE RIGHT WAY

Run from temptations that capture young people. Always do the right thing.

2 TIMOTHY 2:22A CEV

When you are tempted, you really, really want to do something you know you shouldn't. Whether it's sneaking an extra piece of candy or lying to get out of trouble, temptation can be hard to resist! So God says we should "run from temptation."

Sometimes that means actually leaving a place where you feel tempted—like walking away from the candy bowl or from friends who tell lies. You can also pray for courage to do the right thing, even when it's hard. Keep practicing good choices, and it'll get easier to turn down temptation.

THOUGHT OF THE DAY

When do you get tempted? Make a plan! How will you "run from temptation" next time?

PRAY TODAY

Dear God, sometimes I really want to do things I shouldn't do. Please help me run from temptation and do what's right! Amen.

A SAFE PLACE

You are my hiding place and my shield; I hope in your word.

PSALM 119:114 NCV

What makes you feel safe? A hug from someone you love? Holding a favorite toy? How about saying a prayer?

Today's verse tells us that God is a protector. Sometimes people go through hard times and the world feels scary. Thinking about God's good promises can help you feel safe. His love never goes away, no matter what's happening around us or what mistakes we make. So when you feel nervous or lonely or angry or sad, remember that you are wrapped in God's love. He is a safe place that goes wherever you go.

THOUGHT OF THE DAY

God is always with you—you can't accidentally leave Him at home!

PRAY TODAY

Dear God, I am glad You're with me all the time. Please hold me close when I feel scared. Amen.

THANK YOU!

Give thanks to the LORD, for he is good! His faithful love endures forever.

PSALM 136:1 NLT

People love to receive thank you notes when they send a gift. A thoughtful note lets them know you enjoy their gift! God likes to know you enjoy His good gifts too. So why not send Him a note?

Draw a picture of something that makes you happy and thank God while you're coloring it. Do you have a funny pet? Did you get to play in the sunshine today, or splash in big rain puddles? God loves to fill your days with good things. Thank Him for a few of them today!

THOUGHT OF THE DAY

Thanking God each day makes you feel good too!

PRAY TODAY

Dear God, what a beautiful world You've made! Thank You for today! Amen.

WISE WORDS

When you're kind to others, you help yourself; when you're cruel to others, you hurt yourself.

PROVERBS 11:17 MSG

Almost three thousand years ago, a wise king named Solomon collected true sayings and wrote them down. The book of Proverbs contains many of these words of wisdom. In fact, today's Bible verse is one of Solomon's sayings!

You might think that being kind only helps the person you are kind to. But a wise person knows that others often treat you the way you treat them. If you want others to be kind to you, be kind to them! It was true three thousand years ago and it's still true today!

THOUGHT OF THE DAY

Be a friend to have a friend!

PRAY TODAY

Dear God, thank You for the wisdom You show me in the Bible. Please help me to follow wise words. Amen.

REAL FAITH

In the same way, faith by itself, if it is not accompanied by action, is dead.

JAMES 2:17 NIV

If someone says they are your friend, you expect them to act like a friend. If you say someone is your friend, they expect you to act like a friend too. We prove our friendship by what we do.

Faith is like that too. When we say we love and believe in God and His Son, Jesus, then our actions should prove it. How? By doing the things Jesus says to do. Tell the truth. Be kind. Treat others the way you want to be treated. We show that our faith is real through the things we do, not just the words we say.

THOUGHT OF THE DAY

What is something you can do today to prove your faith is real?

PRAY TODAY

Dear God, please help me act and speak in ways that show my faith is real. Amen.

WANT OR NEED

"So don't worry at all about having enough food and clothing. . . . But your heavenly Father already knows perfectly well that you need them, and he will give them to you if you give him first place in your life and live as he wants you to."

MATTHEW 6:31–33 TLB

God knows everything about you. He knows your favorite color, your best friend, and your biggest dreams. He knows everything you want! But more importantly, He knows exactly what you need.

When you put God first, He promises to give you the things you need to live the life He's planned for you. So don't worry about having the newest books or the biggest toys. Instead, try to follow God the very best you can. God knows what you need, and He will always take care of you!

THOUGHT OF THE DAY

Think of something you want and something you need. How are they different?

PRAY TODAY

Dear God, help me remember that You will give me everything I need. Amen.

GOD'S PLANS FOR YOU

"The LORD who saved me from a lion and a bear will save me from this Philistine."

1 SAMUEL 17:37A NCV

David was a famous warrior and king. But he didn't start out that way. When David was young, he spent his days alone, taking care of smelly sheep! It was a dirty, boring, and sometimes scary job.

But God knew something David didn't. God knew that one day David would need the skills he used to protect his sheep to become a brave king who could protect God's people. God knows your future too, and He can use what you are learning now to help you become the person He wants you to be! God has exciting plans for you!

THOUGHT OF THE DAY

Grow and learn all that you can, so you can do what God has planned!

PRAY TODAY

Dear God, I don't know what You have planned for me, but You do. Help me get ready! Amen.

KEEP ON BURNING!

Don't burn out; keep yourselves fueled and aflame. Be alert servants of the Master, cheerfully expectant. Don't quit in hard times; pray all the harder.

ROMANS 12:11–12 MSG

A fire can keep you warm on a cold night or light up a dark room. God says that we should be like a warm, bright fire! Then we can help others feel God's comfort and shine a light to show them how to follow Him. And just like a fire needs wood to keep on burning, you need fuel to stay strong!

What kind of fuel does a person need? Healthy food helps your body grow. Spending time with friends and family helps you love others well. And plenty of time with God will keep you joyful and courageous. So fuel up! Then you'll be ready for anything.

THOUGHT OF THE DAY

Don't run out of fuel. Make time for God every day!

PRAY TODAY

Dear God, thank You for being my fuel! Help me keep on burning for You every day. Amen.

DAY 104

WHAT DO YOU TRUST?

"But blessed are those who trust in the LORD and have made the LORD their hope and confidence."

JEREMIAH 17:7 NLT

People put their trust in all kinds of different things. Some people trust in their brains or their muscles. Some people trust in the things they own or being popular. When you trust in something, you are counting on it to always be there for you.

But guess what? Brains, muscles, what you own, and popularity can all change. Trusting in something that can change is risky. But do you know what never changes? God! And God says if you trust in Him you will always have blessings. God will always be there for you!

THOUGHT OF THE DAY

Why can you always trust in God?

PRAY TODAY

Dear God, thank You for being trustworthy. I am so glad I can always count on You. Amen.

HOPE IN GOD

Let your unfailing love surround us, LORD, for our hope is in you alone.

PSALM 33:22 NLT

Putting your hope in something means you need that thing to make you happy. People put their hope in all kinds of things—money or being famous or even other people! The problem is, all those things can change. But do you know what never changes? God's love!

So why not put your hope in God instead? That means you trust Him to take care of you. You know He is in control, no matter what happens. And you believe Him when He promises that He has good plans for you. When things don't go the way you want, no problem! God has your hope, and nothing can take it away!

THOUGHT OF THE DAY

Hope in God and you will see. He'll take care of you and me!

PRAY TODAY

Dear God, thank You that I can put my hope in You. I love You. Amen.

THE BEST KIND OF LOVE

"As the Father has loved Me, I have also loved you. Remain in My love."

JOHN 15:9 HCSB

Jesus loves us with a special kind of love called "unconditional love." That means His love doesn't depend on the things you've done or will do—it's already yours, forever!

His love is always patient, always kind, and always forgiving. He never gets tired of hearing from you, and you can talk to Him about anything! In fact, that's the best way to feel His love and become friends with Him. So spend some time with Him today. Jesus can be your very best friend, because He has the very best kind of love.

THOUGHT OF THE DAY

Jesus loved you yesterday, He loves you today, and He'll love you tomorrow!

PRAY TODAY

Dear Jesus, I love to think about Your amazing love. Let's become best friends! Amen.

BEAUTIFUL FRIENDS

I will praise You because I have been remarkably and wonderfully made. Your works are wonderful, and I know this very well.

PSALM 139:14 HCSB

No two people are exactly alike. Look around! God filled His world with people of different sizes, colors, interests, and abilities.

You might know someone who needs a little extra help. People who need help learning often have a special helper. People who need help getting around might have a wheelchair or crutches. People who need help seeing can wear glasses or use a special cane. Someone who looks, sounds, or acts differently from you can be just as good a friend as anyone else! So be sure to include all kinds of people when you're making friends. It'll make your world even more beautiful!

THOUGHT OF THE DAY

Sometimes people feel sensitive about differences. Be sure to ask questions with kindness!

PRAY TODAY

Dear God, thank You for making all sorts of amazing people! Amen.

DAY 108

GOD IS IN CONTROL

So we will not be afraid even if the earth shakes, or the mountains fall into the sea.

PSALM 46:2 NCV

The Bible tells us that God is in control of everything. But that doesn't mean He controls all our choices. Nope, we still get to decide how to act and what to say. So sometimes we get hurt or hurt other people. But no matter what, God always cares for us. His love doesn't depend on good days or bad days. You never have to be afraid, because He can bring good things out of anything. God is always good, always with you, and always in charge.

THOUGHT OF THE DAY

Some days can feel sad or even scary. God can help you through them all.

PRAY TODAY

Dear God, I'm glad I can count on You, no matter what happens. Amen.

THE GIFT OF YES

Do everything without complaining and arguing.

PHILIPPIANS 2:14 NLT

You can give a wonderful gift to someone, and it won't cost a penny. Do you know what it is? The gift of Yes! Here's how it works. The next time someone asks for your help, just say "Yes!" Don't argue about doing it later or complain about how much you don't want to. Say yes and help right away! Then watch what happens. Chances are you'll get a big smile, a big thank-you, and maybe even a big hug! When you help people with a cheerful attitude, they feel loved and important. What a wonderful—and simple!—gift to give.

THOUGHT OF THE DAY

Who can you surprise with a "Yes!" today?

PRAY TODAY

Dear God, help me always to be a cheerful helper. Amen.

THINK LIKE GOD

Don't be like the people of this world, but let God change the way you think. Then you will know how to do everything that is good and pleasing to him.

ROMANS 12:2 CEV

Some kids like to tell others what to do. What if someone says you can't be friends with someone else? Or tells you to call another kid a mean name? Do you have to do what they say?

No! God gave you a good mind, and you can use it to make good, safe decisions! That might be hard when you really want to impress a friend or make your classmates laugh. But God can help you. Ask God to make your thoughts more like His. When you think like God, you'll know the right choice to make.

THOUGHT OF THE DAY

Has someone ever told you to do something wrong? How did you feel?

PRAY TODAY

Dear God, I know what's right and what's wrong. Help me think more like You so I always choose what's right. Amen.

UNIQUELY YOU

Something from the Spirit can be seen in each person, to help everyone.

1 CORINTHIANS 12:7 ICB

Nobody looks, sounds, or even thinks the same. That's because God gave everyone different gifts so we can all help each other! Do you read well? Read your sister a bedtime story! Love flowers? Plant some blooms to brighten your front yard. Are you good at video games? Help a friend learn to beat a tough level!

But what about things you're not good at? Those are important too! When you ask someone for help, they get to share their special gifts with you. What a fun world God gave us—there is so much to learn and share!

THOUGHT OF THE DAY

What do you think is one of your gifts? What gifts do you see in others?

PRAY TODAY

Dear God, each person has something special to give. Help me find mine, and to enjoy others' too! Amen.

SHOW THEM GOD

For though we have never yet seen God, when we love each other God lives in us, and his love within us grows ever stronger.

1 JOHN 4:12 TLB

No one can see God. But you can still show people what God looks like. How? Share His love!

The Bible says that love comes from God. So people see a little bit of Him whenever we love each other well! You can do that by letting others go first, helping people in need, and sharing your gifts with the world. When you decide to be generous, you show that God cares for everyone. When you choose patient words instead of angry ones, you show how God treats us. You are a little bit of God walking around—show Him off!

THOUGHT OF THE DAY

Who will you love today?

PRAY TODAY

Dear God, please help me show someone what You look like today! I want to love like You do. Amen.

FRIENDS AND FAMILY

Friends come and friends go, but a true friend sticks by you like family.

PROVERBS 18:24 MSG

It's fun to share happy times with good friends! But what makes someone a great friend? A great friend is someone you can do hard things with too. If you make a mistake, you can apologize and ask forgiveness—and they can do the same. You can talk honestly if you get upset with each other. When you need help, a great friend steps in. And if you have a sad day, the best kinds of friends stick around and help you feel better. You can turn good friends into great friends by being the kind of friend you want to have.

THOUGHT OF THE DAY

Friends are gifts from God. Take care of yours!

PRAY TODAY

Dear God, help me be a great friend! Amen.

DAY 114

HOME WITH GOD

"May your kingdom come and what you want be done, here on earth as it is in heaven."

MATTHEW 6:10 NCV

The Bible tells us that heaven is a wonderful place. There is no meanness or loneliness, and everyone knows God's love. When you choose to follow Jesus, He invites you to live with Him in heaven forever!

But we shouldn't just sit around waiting for heaven. Instead, Jesus wants us to bring a little heaven to earth! Share God's love every day. Notice when other kids are lonely and invite them to play. When someone needs help, step in without being asked! Give away things you don't need, and be generous with kind words too. Every loving act shines God's heavenly light.

THOUGHT OF THE DAY

Make your home feel a little like heaven, so heaven will feel just like home!

PRAY TODAY

Dear God, I'm glad I get to spend forever with You in heaven. Until then, help me show others what Your home will be like! Amen.

FREEDOM FROM ANGER

"When you are praying, if you are angry with someone, forgive him so that your Father in heaven will also forgive your sins."

MARK 11:25 NCV

Have you ever been angry with someone? Maybe they hurt your feelings or did something you thought was unfair. God understands how you feel, but He also wants you to be free from those angry feelings.

The Bible says that if we forgive others, God forgives us! When you forgive the person who makes you angry, you let go of your angry feelings and make room for God's forgiveness to fill your heart instead. A heart filled with forgiveness is much better than a heart filled with anger. Try it! You'll be glad you did.

THOUGHT OF THE DAY

Who might you need to forgive today?

PRAY TODAY

Dear God, please help me forgive others so I can be free from anger. Thanks for forgiving me too. Amen.

ALL-THE-TIME LOVE

And so we know the love that God has for us, and we trust that love.

1 JOHN 4:16A ICB

There are lots of different kinds of love. You might love your friends or your school or your soccer team. Or pizza and ice cream! But some loves change. Some days you're not in the mood for pizza. Maybe you'll stop liking ice cream! You might change schools or teams or even friendships. But one love always stays the same: God's love.

God has always loved you, and He always will. He loves you when you're happy, angry, silly, or sad. Nothing you do can change God's love for you. Wherever you go—and whatever you eat!—He loves you all the time.

THOUGHT OF THE DAY

Summer, winter, spring, or fall, God will love you through it all.

PRAY TODAY

Dear God, Your love is bigger than anything. Thank You for loving me all the time! Amen.

WHAT'S YOUR CHOICE?

"Do everything the LORD your God requires. Live the way he wants you to. Obey his orders and commands."

1 KINGS 2:3A NIRV

It can feel like grown-ups decide everything. After all, a grown-up usually picks what's for dinner, tells you when to turn off screens, and sets your bedtime. So, what choices do YOU get to make?

Really important ones! Every day, you get to decide how you'll follow God. Often, that looks like how you treat other people. Will you be generous or selfish when a friend asks to play? Will you sit next to a new classmate or ignore her? Will you look for ways to help your family or complain about doing chores? Each day is filled with choices. What will yours be?

THOUGHT OF THE DAY

Can you think of a choice you made yesterday?

PRAY TODAY

Dear God, I want to live the way You want me to. Help me make good choices! Amen.

DOING WHAT GOD WANTS

"Seek first God's kingdom and what God wants. Then all your other needs will be met as well."

MATTHEW 6:33 NCV

One day Jesus listened to some people who were worried. "What about us?" they asked. "How will we get what we need?" Jesus told them that if they did what God wanted first, they could stop worrying because God would take care of them. That's good advice for us too. The Bible teaches us what God wants us to do: be kind, share what you have, make everyone feel welcomed, help people who are hurting or sad, pray for others. Doing what God wants first takes care of everyone's needs—including yours!

THOUGHT OF THE DAY

What is something God wants you to do today?

PRAY TODAY

Dear God, please help me to do what You want and to trust You for all I need. Amen.

GOD'S ANGELS

For he will order his angels to protect you wherever you go.

PSALM 91:11 NLT

Have you ever dressed up like an angel? Did you wear wings and a glittery halo? In the Bible angels don't always look like that. Sometimes they are even invisible!

Angels are special messengers sent from God to help us. Sometimes we need to feel comforted when we are sad. Sometimes we need to choose to be kind. Another time we may need courage when we are afraid.

The Bible says that God's angels are always with us. They help us, protect us, and remind us of God's love. The next time you feel alone, remember that God's angels are with you, and they will help you!

THOUGHT OF THE DAY

God protects you every day, sending love in every way!

PRAY TODAY

Dear God, thank You for all the ways You love and care for me. Please surround me with Your angels! Amen.

DAY 120

LEAD WITH YOUR ACTIONS

In every way be an example of doing good deeds. When you teach, do it with honesty and seriousness.

TITUS 2:7 NCV

The best leaders don't just tell others what to do—they lead with their actions! And God wants you to lead people to Him. So be sure to choose good, kind actions that show people what God's love looks like! Treat people with respect, and they'll understand how to treat others that way too. When you keep your promises, you show what it means to be trustworthy, even when it's hard. When you tell the truth, others can see what honesty looks like. How will you lead with your actions today?

THOUGHT OF THE DAY

You can be a leader by following God's ways!

PRAY TODAY

Dear God, help me choose good actions so I can be a good leader who points people to You! Amen.

DAY 121

PRAY YOUR WORRY AWAY

Don't worry about anything; instead, pray about everything. Tell God what you need, and thank him for all he has done.

PHILIPPIANS 4:6 NLT

When you're worrying, it's hard to think of anything else! So the Bible gives us an easy prayer that can help: tell God what you need and thank Him for all He's done.

Sometimes people forget that last part. They tell God what they want but they forget to say thanks. Thanking God isn't only polite—it's also helpful! When you spend time remembering the good things God has done, there's less time to think about what's bothering you. It also reminds you that God will do good things again. So when worries start to fill your mind, stop and pray those worries away!

THOUGHT OF THE DAY

What's worrying you today? Stop and pray!

PRAY TODAY

Dear God, please help me remember Your goodness, so I can stop worrying and start trusting! Amen.

DAY 122

GOD IS ALWAYS WITH YOU

"Do not be afraid or discouraged. For the LORD your God is with you wherever you go."

JOSHUA 1:9 NLT

What's the most interesting place you have ever visited? Have you been to the zoo or a museum? Maybe you have traveled to another state or even to a foreign country. Would you ever like to go into outer space? Do you know that no matter where you go, God is with you? Even if you were able to live on the moon, God would be there!

You can't always be with your parents or friends, but you can always be with God. That's why you don't have to be afraid or discouraged. God is with you wherever you go!

THOUGHT OF THE DAY

Try to name all the places God will be with you today.

PRAY TODAY

Dear God, I'm so glad You are always with me. Thank You for loving me so much. Amen.

LISTEN CAREFULLY!

Listen carefully to wisdom; set your mind on understanding.

PROVERBS 2:2 NCV

Sometimes it's SO hard to listen to grown-ups. A lot of times they're telling you what to do, right? And you might want to do something else!

But guess what? Having good, loving grown-ups in your life is a special gift from God. That's because grown-ups have lots of wisdom to share—they've already been kids, so they know what it's like! Try to listen to what they tell you. And if it's hard to listen, try telling them that too! Together, you can work on ways to talk and listen to each other.

THOUGHT OF THE DAY

"Advice" is a piece of wisdom that's easy to remember. Ask a grown-up for their favorite piece of advice!

PRAY TODAY

Dear God, help me listen carefully to the loving grown-ups You've given me. I want to learn wisdom! Amen.

DAY 124

FAITH BRICKS

So faith comes from hearing, and hearing through the word of Christ.

ROMANS 10:17 ESV

Faith means you trust God's love and help, even though you can't see Him. If you want a strong faith, all you have to do is build it!

But how? Just like you build a house with many small bricks, you can build your faith with many small "faith bricks." Faith comes from hearing God's truth, so listening to Bible stories is a great way to gather faith bricks! When you ask good questions about Jesus, you're adding even more. And each time you pray, you add another brick to your faith tower. So keep building! With a strong faith, you can do big things.

THOUGHT OF THE DAY

Brick by brick, your faith grows tall. No small thing will make it fall.

PRAY TODAY

Dear God, help me build a strong faith in You so I can have courage, share Your love, and do big things. Amen.

ASK AND GROW

. . . so that you will live the kind of life that honors and pleases the Lord in every way. You will produce fruit in every good work and grow in the knowledge of God.

COLOSSIANS 1:10 NCV

Do you have a lot of questions about God? That's great! The Bible says we can always learn something new about His wonderful ways.

You can learn from Bible stories and listening to teachers and pastors. God can also help you find answers when you pray. As you spend more time with God, you might realize you want to know even more! So keep asking questions—God gave you a curious mind that can wonder and imagine. Don't be afraid to use it!

THOUGHT OF THE DAY

Even grown-ups are still learning. See if you can work together to discover something new!

PRAY TODAY

Dear God, I hope I always want to know more about You! Thank You for my curious mind. Amen.

HAPPINESS FROM THE INSIDE

I'm happy from the inside out, and from the outside in, I'm firmly formed.

PSALM 16:9A MSG

A smile often means a happy heart! But sometimes people put on a smile when they feel angry inside. Or they act happy when they are really sad. Or they hide their scared feelings by acting extra loud and silly. They think they need to pretend so others will like them.

When it's hard for you to feel happy all the way through, ask God to help you understand why. Find a grown-up who will listen to your feelings, and help you find good solutions. You are precious to God. He wants your outside happiness to come from inside joy!

THOUGHT OF THE DAY

How does your inside feel?

PRAY TODAY

Dear God, please help me pay attention to my inside feelings, and please give me Your joy! Amen.

GET THE ICKIES OUT

Tell your sins to each other. And pray for each other so you may be healed.

JAMES 5:16A NLV

Can you remember a time you made a mistake or a poor choice? Maybe you broke something or hurt someone's feelings. It can feel icky inside when that happens. You might want to pretend it didn't happen. But God has a different idea.

God asks us to tell each other when we've done something wrong. That's because something cool happens when you're brave enough to tell the truth: it gets the ickies out! Start by saying sorry, but don't stop there. Ask how to make things better, and how to make safe, helpful choices next time! You'll be icky-less in no time!

THOUGHT OF THE DAY

If it's scary to share your mistakes, find a grown-up who can help you!

PRAY TODAY

Dear God, it's sometimes hard to tell the truth. Help me be brave, so I can send those icky feelings far away! Amen.

PEACEFUL FRIENDSHIPS

It is good and pleasant when God's people live together in peace!

PSALM 133:1 NCV

What kinds of people do you like to be around? Loud and exciting? Quiet and thoughtful? A bit of both? All friendships are different, but the best friendships are peaceful ones.

Peace means no matter what you do, you find ways to be kind to one another. If you get upset with a friend, you don't yell or fight—you talk about it. Nobody tells lies or says mean things. Instead, you only say good things to AND about each other! God says that when you fill your friendships with peace, you'll have so much more fun!

THOUGHT OF THE DAY

The key to good friendships is not hard to find. It's the peace that you feel when you choose to be kind!

PRAY TODAY

Dear God, if my friends and I disagree, help me to always make the choice that will lead to peace. Amen.

WHO DO YOU SEE?

Do you not know that you are the temple of God and that the Spirit of God dwells in you?

1 CORINTHIANS 3:16 NKJV

When you think about yourself, what do you see? Do you see the things you do well or the things that need work? Do you think about the last time you got in trouble or that funny joke you told? Do you like the person you're thinking about?

Here's what God sees: someone He loves very much. He will always rejoice in your happy times and help you through hard things. But He loves you exactly the way you are right now. You don't need to change anything to earn God's love: you already have it! So next time you look in the mirror, try to see what God sees: a beloved child!

THOUGHT OF THE DAY

Short or tall, brown eyes or blue, God loves what He sees in you!

PRAY TODAY

Dear God, thank You for loving me just the way I am! Help me love myself that way too. Amen.

DO THE RIGHT THING

He grants a treasure of common sense to the honest. He is a shield to those who walk with integrity.

PROVERBS 2:7 NLT

Life is full of rules, isn't it? If someone sees you breaking a rule, you might get in trouble. But what if no one knows? What if you feel like breaking a rule, and you think no one will notice? Don't do it! God sees, and He wants you to make good choices.

When you do the right thing, even when no one notices, that's called integrity. Maybe you tell the truth even when lying is easier. You clean your mess because you promised to, even if no one is watching. When you live with integrity, you can be proud of yourself every day!

THOUGHT OF THE DAY

Integrity is a gift you give to yourself.

PRAY TODAY

Dear God, sometimes I get tired of following rules. Help me choose integrity even when I don't feel like it. Amen.

A HAPPY HEART

Every day is hard for those who suffer, but a happy heart is like a continual feast.

PROVERBS 15:15 NCV

Have you ever noticed how some people always seem to complain about things? "This lunch looks yucky!" "I don't like this shirt." "My chores are too hard." "I never get what I want."

Maybe you also know some friends who always seem cheerful. "Hey, it's raining, but I love puddles!" "This isn't my favorite, but that's OK." "Here, you can have the bigger cookie!"

Which sounds better to you? Today's Bible verse says you'll have more fun when you choose cheerfulness. So next time you feel like complaining, say something happy instead. Then see how it makes you feel!

THOUGHT OF THE DAY

Think of three things you're happy about today.

PRAY TODAY

Dear God, will You please help me to have a cheerful heart? I want to learn to look for ways to spread happiness. Amen.

DAY 132

BE SMART AND WISE

Are there those among you who are truly wise and understanding? Then they should show it by living right and doing good things with a gentleness that comes from wisdom.

JAMES 3:13A NCV

Do you know the difference between being smart and being wise? Being smart means that you know things, like math, music, or spelling. Being wise means you use what you know to do what is right and good.

If you can solve math problems well, use that skill to help others. If you can play an instrument or sing, use your music to bring joy to someone. If you can write or draw well, create art that blesses others. Be creative! Ask God to help you find ways to be both smart AND wise.

THOUGHT OF THE DAY

How are you using something you know in a way that is wise?

PRAY TODAY

Dear God, thank You that I am learning so many new things. Please help me also learn how to be wise. Amen.

KEEP ON GOING

But endurance must do its complete work, so that you may be mature and complete, lacking nothing.

JAMES 1:4 HCSB

Endurance is a long word that means "to keep on going." If you have endurance, you don't give up when things are hard. If you are learning to ride a bike, but you give up the first time you fall off, you'll never learn to ride. If you quit drawing pictures when they don't turn out the way you like, you won't learn how to draw better.

Endurance helps us become better at all sorts of things—from music to sports to friendships. It also helps us learn how to finish work that is hard. So ask God to help you endure. It's a gift worth working for!

THOUGHT OF THE DAY

What is a skill or task you need endurance to complete?

PRAY TODAY

Dear God, help me not to get discouraged when things don't work out the first time I try. Please help me to keep on going. Amen.

LOOK STRAIGHT AHEAD

Let your eyes look straight ahead; fix your gaze directly before you.

PROVERBS 4:25 NIV

Imagine you're running in a race. You're having a great time! Then suddenly, you start to worry. Where's everyone else? Are they faster than me? Am I winning? So you turn and look. Sure enough, you find the other runners, but looking around makes you swerve and slow down—maybe even trip and fall! If you had kept your eyes straight ahead, you would have run a better race.

Your life is like that race. God has wonderful plans for each of us. Don't spend time worrying that someone else will be better at one thing or another. Instead trust God to lead you, and keep your eyes on Him!

THOUGHT OF THE DAY

When you're looking at God, you're going the right way!

PRAY TODAY

Dear God, thank You for making a path for me. Please help me when I compare myself with other people. Amen.

STRONGER THAN TEMPTATION

"Stay awake and pray for strength against temptation. The spirit wants to do what is right, but the body is weak."

MATTHEW 26:41 NCV

Temptation is when you know you shouldn't do something, but you really really want to. Have you ever felt that way? You know what's right, but the wrong choice just looks easier or more fun . . . or both!

God says you need strength to fight against temptation. One way to get stronger is to make a plan! Decide what you'll do next time you feel tempted. Will you ask for help? Will you walk away from the cookie jar or from kids who are teasing someone else? Ask God for ideas. With His strength, temptation won't stand a chance!

THOUGHT OF THE DAY

Even Jesus faced temptation—He can help you be strong too!

PRAY TODAY

Dear God, sometimes it's hard to choose the right thing. Please give me strength when I'm tempted. Amen.

SHARING GROWS!

"If you have two shirts, share with the person who does not have one. If you have food, share that too."

LUKE 3:11 ICB

So many great things happen when you share! First, you are taking care of others. You might have something that someone else really needs and you can bless them by sharing it. Second, you're acting in a loving way. Whenever you do that, you show people a little bit of what God looks like. How cool is that? Third, you might inspire them to share with someone else. That means your kindness could help people you don't even know! And finally, joy, love, and peace will grow in your heart. So get out there and share!

THOUGHT OF THE DAY

Don't be surprised if sharing once makes you want to share even more!

PRAY TODAY

Dear God, thank You for all the ways You've blessed me. Help me share those blessings with others. Amen.

FOCUS ON YOU

Be kind to one another, tenderhearted, forgiving one another, as God in Christ forgave you.

EPHESIANS 4:32 ESV

You can't change the way anyone else acts. But you don't have to. Instead, God wants you to focus on yourself. What can YOU do to help others and show love?

One of the most important things you can do is to be kind to everyone. Even people you don't like. Even when someone is mean to you. Even when your little sister breaks a toy you told her not to touch. Your actions might change the way others behave, or they might not. But choosing kindness every day will change you!

THOUGHT OF THE DAY

God is working on your heart. Trust Him to work on everyone else's too!

PRAY TODAY

Dear God, please help me focus on my own actions instead of anyone else's. Thank You for helping me grow each day! Amen.

EVERYDAY MIRACLES

"God can do anything!"

LUKE 1:37 NCV

Sometimes when we think about the amazing things God does, we imagine Him creating billions of stars, gigantic oceans, or enormous mountains. It is easy to overlook the miracles God does every day. Every tiny seed that sprouts is a miracle! It is a miracle that your body works the way it does. It's a miracle that you can invent and imagine new ideas. It is a miracle when God helps you forgive someone or changes a wrong attitude to be right. Nothing is too big or small for God to do because He can do anything!

THOUGHT OF THE DAY

Name some everyday miracles you see!

PRAY TODAY

Dear God, thank You for creating the world and everything in it. I'm so glad You can do anything! Amen.

CONTROL YOURSELF

Losing self-control leaves you as helpless as a city without a wall.

PROVERBS 25:28 CEV

In Bible times, people built large walls around their cities to keep enemies and wild animals out. A city without a wall was in danger. Today's Bible verse says that a person who loses self-control is also in danger. When you control your temper, you don't say or do things that might hurt yourself or someone else. And when you use self-control and follow the rules at school or in your neighborhood, you keep yourself and others safe. Can you think of some other ways that learning to control yourself will help avoid danger?

THOUGHT OF THE DAY

Make it your goal to show self-control!

PRAY TODAY

Dear Lord, I'm so glad You love me and want me to be safe. Please help me practice self-control. Amen.

FRIENDS FOREVER

Jesus Christ is the same yesterday and today and forever.

HEBREWS 13:8 ESV

Friends are a wonderful gift from God! It's fun to find people who like the same things you do. Some friendships last for years, and some only last a short time. Friends might move away or just decide they like different things. Everyone grows and changes, and that means friendships grow and change too. But one friend will never change: Jesus. He has always loved you, even before you were born. He will always be with you. He will guide you and hear your prayers wherever you go. No matter what happens, you and Jesus will be friends forever!

THOUGHT OF THE DAY

How does it feel to know Jesus is your friend?

PRAY TODAY

Dear Jesus, thank You for being my very best friend forever! Amen.

ALL IN THE FAMILY

His unchanging plan has always been to adopt us into his own family by sending Jesus Christ to die for us. And he did this because he wanted to!

EPHESIANS 1:5 TLB

No two families are the same. But every family is a gift from God! You might not feel that way when you're arguing with your little brother or when your dad gives you extra chores. But the people in your life help you grow into the person God wants you to be. Everyone in a family is important. We have unique gifts and personalities, and we can help each other in different ways.

In fact, family is so important that God sent Jesus so that we could all be part of His family too! With God as our Father, we will always be loved, cherished, and cared for.

THOUGHT OF THE DAY

Find a way to help your family today!

PRAY TODAY

Dear God, I love being in Your family! Thank You for all the ways You care for me. Amen.

IT'S FUN TO BE KIND

Finally, all of you, be like-minded, be sympathetic, love one another, be compassionate and humble.

1 PETER 3:8 NIV

You know that God asks you to be kind. But did you also know that being kind can be fun?

Do you like to draw? Make cards for all your neighbors or help a friend draw something new. Can you read? Read a book to a younger sibling while your mom and dad are making dinner. Is there someone who always sits alone at recess? Invite him or her to play with you. See how fast you can clean up a mess without being asked. Tell someone your favorite thing about them! Be kind any chance you get. Then don't be surprised if others join the fun too!

THOUGHT OF THE DAY

What's your favorite way to be kind?

PRAY TODAY

Dear God, I'm glad there are so many ways to be kind. Help me show everyone how fun it can be! Amen.

GOD IS THERE FOR YOU

"The LORD himself will fight for you. Just stay calm."

EXODUS 14:14 NLT

It's easy to trust God when everything is fun and easy. But what if you're scared? There was a time in the Bible when Moses helped God's people escape from their enemies. But when their enemies chased after them, God's people were terrified! Then Moses reminded them that God was with them, and He would fight for them. They only needed to calm down and trust God.

Do you know that God is always there for you too? When you're facing something that makes you afraid, ask God to help you be calm and trust Him.

THOUGHT OF THE DAY

Whenever you don't know what to do, remember God is there for you!

PRAY TODAY

Dear God, I'm so thankful that You are here for me! Please help me remember to call on You whenever I'm afraid. Amen.

THE BEST LISTENER

I cried to him for help; I praised him with songs.

PSALM 66:17 GNT

At church, you might hear all kinds of prayers. Sometimes people use a lot of fancy words to pray. Other times, they sound like they're talking with a good friend. Prayers can sound sad or joyful or even confused and angry. Sometimes people ask God for things, and sometimes they just tell God how wonderful He is. They might even do both in the same prayer! God listens to each and every kind of prayer.

No matter how you're feeling, you can always talk to God. You don't have to know any special words. God will always listen to you.

THOUGHT OF THE DAY

God loves to hear your prayers. Talk to Him today!

PRAY TODAY

Dear God, thank You for always caring about me and listening to all my prayers. Amen.

LOVE EVERYONE?

"There is a saying, 'Love your friends and hate your enemies.' But I say: Love your enemies! Pray for those who persecute you!"

MATTHEW 5:43–44 TLB

Has someone ever been mean to you? That feels pretty rotten. Maybe you even thought about being mean to them in return.

But Jesus tells us to do something else: love and pray for people who are mean to you! That's not just surprising, it's HARD. So ask for God's help. Sometimes people are mean because they are unhappy—try praying for happiness in that person's life. Plan for how you will choose kindness toward them. You don't have to become best friends. But maybe your love and prayers will help them become a little more friendly!

THOUGHT OF THE DAY

Remember that love is an action: you don't have to feel loving to show love to others!

PRAY TODAY

Dear God, will You please show me how to love and pray for everyone, even when they are mean? I need Your help. Amen.

DAY 146

HELP YOUR FRIENDS

You use steel to sharpen steel, and one friend sharpens another.

PROVERBS 27:17 MSG

Knives need to be sharp to do good work. To sharpen a dull knife, a person scrapes the blade along another piece of metal. The pieces of metal help each other!

You have good work to do too. God needs you to be the best YOU that you can be! So He gives you good friends to help you do just that. Good friends help each other learn new things, be brave, and choose kindness. And the best friends gently remind us when we need to fix something we've done wrong. Friends keep each other "sharp" so they can do great things!

THOUGHT OF THE DAY

Can you help a friend make a good choice today?

PRAY TODAY

Dear God, help me be a friend who helps others—and help me choose friends like that too! Amen.

YES, YOU CAN!

"For I am about to do something new. See, I have already begun! Do you not see it?"

ISAIAH 43:19A NLT

Do you like to try new things? Not everyone does! Sometimes it feels scary to try a new game, play with new friends, learn a new instrument, or even just tell someone about a new idea. God says you don't need to feel that way, because anything is possible when you have faith in Him! That doesn't mean you will be instantly perfect at everything you try. It means you can trust God to help you work hard, learn from your mistakes, and grow in confidence. When you depend on God's help, nothing can stop you!

THOUGHT OF THE DAY

What's something new you want to try?

PRAY TODAY

Dear God, sometimes I feel scared or embarrassed to try new things. Please help me remember to trust in Your help! Amen.

A MAP TO GOD

Jesus answered, "I am the way and the truth and the life. No one comes to the Father except through me."

JOHN 14:6 NIV

For a long time, people wondered what God was like. They wanted to get to know Him better, but they didn't know how. Then one day, God sent Jesus.

Jesus was God walking on earth! When Jesus came, no one had to wonder what God was like anymore—they could follow Him around! And you can do that too. When you feel like God is hard to understand, remember Jesus' life. He helped people who were different from Him, shared what He had, and loved everyone. Following Jesus closely is the best way to get close to God!

THOUGHT OF THE DAY

Jesus is like a secret passage to God's heart!

PRAY TODAY

Dear God, thank You for sending Jesus so I can understand You better and love You even more! Amen.

COURAGE WHEN YOU FEEL AFRAID

Wait for the LORD; be strong, and let your heart take courage.

PSALM 27:14A ESV

Do you think heroes ever feel afraid? They do! Just look in the Bible. Esther risked her life to save her family, but she spent three whole days praying for help first. Barak was a great soldier, but he only agreed to fight a big battle if his friend Deborah came along. Even Jesus felt scared before He was arrested! Real courage means doing the right thing, even when you feel afraid.

What's hard for you to feel brave about? God doesn't expect you to do hard things alone. Ask Him for help, then trust Him to give you the courage you need.

THOUGHT OF THE DAY

Next time you feel nervous, stop, pray, and trust. You can be a hero too!

PRAY TODAY

Dear God, when I feel scared, I want to run and hide. Help me stop and pray for courage instead. Amen.

ALWAYS WITH YOU

"The eyes of the LORD watch over those who do right, and his ears are open to their prayers."

1 PETER 3:12 NLT

Do you know that you are never alone? Even when your family can't be with you. Even when your best friend isn't there. Even when you might feel like you are all alone, there is Someone right beside you. You are never alone because Jesus is always there.

The Bible says that Jesus sees what is going on. He knows what you are going through. He loves you and always hears your prayers. So, the next time you feel lonely or like no one understands, remember this promise: you always have a Friend with you. Jesus sees and hears you!

THOUGHT OF THE DAY

How can Jesus help you when you feel alone?

PRAY TODAY

Dear God, thank You for Your promise to always see and hear me. Please help me remember that I am never alone. Amen.

BIG AND SMALL

"Remembering the words the Lord Jesus himself said: 'It is more blessed to give than to receive.'"

ACTS 20:35B NIV

How do you feel when you help people? Do you feel happy when you work hard to make a special gift for your grandma or cheer loudly for a friend? Doing good things can feel great! Sometimes it may seem like your small decisions don't matter. Does anyone care that you're keeping your promises each day, or not sharing gossip, or sitting with a friend who feels left out? Yes! God cares! You make the world better with every good choice, and God is so proud of you. Keep choosing good actions, big and small. Everything you do matters!

THOUGHT OF THE DAY

Doing good is a big deal—even when it's something small!

PRAY TODAY

Dear God, sometimes I forget to make good choices in the small things. Help me do good things of every size, every day! Amen.

FOLLOW THE DIRECTIONS

Now if you really obey the Lord . . . God will set you high above all nations on the earth.

DEUTERONOMY 28:1 CEB

Larry was so excited about his new construction set! But nothing was working out. He got more and more frustrated. When Bob came by, Larry showed him the messed-up project.

"Did you follow these?" asked Bob, holding up the directions. He sat down with Larry and they carefully followed each step. Soon the project was finished, and it looked great!

God gives us directions in the Bible too! When we ignore them and do things our own way, we often end up disappointed! But when we obey what God says, things always work out better.

THOUGHT OF THE DAY

When we obey, God shows us the way!

PRAY TODAY

Dear God, please help me to obey You so that I can learn the right way to live. Amen.

THE "GREEN-EYED MONSTER"

Don't set your heart on anything that is your neighbor's.

EXODUS 20:17B MSG

Have you ever wanted what someone else has? Let's say your friend has a cool new bike. Suddenly, you don't like your bike anymore. You want your friend's bike instead. Soon, all you can think about is the bike that you don't have. Wanting what someone else has is called envy. Some people call envy "a green-eyed monster!" It's a monster because it gobbles up all your joy and can even ruin friendships. But you can destroy this icky beast! Start thanking God for what you have. List all the blessings you can think of! The "green-eyed monster" of envy will run away from a heart filled with thankfulness.

THOUGHT OF THE DAY

Name five things you're thankful for.

PRAY TODAY

Dear God, I'm so thankful for every blessing I have. Please help me to remember my blessings when I envy others. Amen.

TALKING AND LISTENING

There is a time for everything. . . . a time to be silent and a time to speak.

ECCLESIASTES 3:1, 7 NIV

Do you have a hard time waiting your turn to tell everyone your stories or ideas? Or maybe have a hard time speaking up? Maybe you'd rather listen to a story than tell one. People feel differently about talking in front of others, but God tells us there are times when it's important to be quiet and times when it's important to talk. It is good to know the difference. When you're in school or at church and someone is teaching you, be sure you're a good listener. When you have something important to share, be sure to speak up!

THOUGHT OF THE DAY

What is easier for you—talking or listening?

PRAY TODAY

Thank You, God, for always listening to me. Help me to be a good listener too. Amen.

BRINGING JOY

And a voice from heaven said, "You are my dearly loved Son, and you bring me great joy."

MARK 1:11 NLT

The Bible tells us that Jesus gave God, His Father, great joy. You bring joy to your family too when you speak and act in ways that are good and right. Telling the truth, being kind to others, doing chores without complaining, looking for ways to help, and giving hugs are all simple ways you can show your love for your family.

And when you do these things, you are also bringing joy to God, your heavenly Father! Isn't it great to know that you can make others happy just like Jesus did?

THOUGHT OF THE DAY

What did you do this week to bring joy to the people around you?

PRAY TODAY

Dear God, please help me to be more like Jesus. I want to bring joy to my family. Amen.

DAY 156

GOD'S COMFORT

When doubts filled my mind, your comfort gave me renewed hope and cheer.

PSALM 94:19 NLT

Are you ever afraid? Do you ever wonder about what will happen tomorrow? No person knows everything and no one can tell you exactly what will happen tomorrow. That's why it is so great to know God. He knows all things, and He is not afraid of anything! Whenever you feel afraid or worry about what will happen, you can ask God to help you. He promises to comfort you, to give you hope, and to cheer you up. God is more powerful than your fears and He loves you more than you can even imagine.

THOUGHT OF THE DAY

Give God your doubts and fears, and He will comfort you with hope.

PRAY TODAY

Dear God, thank You for loving me and comforting me when I'm afraid or worried. Amen.

DREAM BIG, TRUST GOD

Now glory be to God, who by his mighty power at work within us is able to do far more than we would ever dare to ask or even dream of—infinitely beyond our highest prayers, desires, thoughts, or hopes.

EPHESIANS 3:20 TLB

Larry likes pretending to be Larryboy—the most super of superheroes! And you probably like to pretend to do exciting things too! But guess what? You can do more than pretend. You can ask God to do mighty things through you. And He will!

He won't make you fly or turn invisible. But God can use you to change the world! Maybe He'll give you super courage to protect a sibling who is getting teased. Or big ideas to help a cause you care about. He'll give you strength to work hard so you can accomplish your biggest dreams. Nothing is too amazing for God!

THOUGHT OF THE DAY

With God, you don't have to pretend. You just have to trust.

PRAY TODAY

Dear God, help me trust You so we can do big things together! Amen.

DAY 158

GOD IS WITH YOU

The LORD is my light and my salvation; Whom shall I fear? The LORD is the strength of my life; Of whom shall I be afraid?

PSALM 27:1 NKJV

The Bible says we never need to be afraid, because God is always with us. But what if you feel scared anyway? Try remembering today's verse.

First, God is your light. If you're feeling confused, imagine God with a giant flashlight. Trust Him, and He'll help you find the right way! Second, God is your salvation. That means no matter what, you always have a home with God. And third, He's your strength. God can help you do big things because He is stronger than any worries. With God by your side, there's nothing to be afraid of.

THOUGHT OF THE DAY

Fears and worries, go away! God is with me every day.

PRAY TODAY

Dear God, when I feel worried or afraid, please remind me that You are near. Amen.

DAY 159

PUT ON YOUR BELT

Stand firm then, with the belt of truth buckled around your waist.

EPHESIANS 6:14A NIV

Did you know that there's something besides your clothes that you should put on every day? The Bible calls it "the belt of truth." That's a word picture describing how God's truth surrounds us and protects us just like a Roman soldier's sword belt.

Jesus said, "I am the Truth!" and Scriptures say that God's Word is true. So we can put on the "belt of truth" every day by following Jesus and memorizing verses from the Bible. Here are some great ones: "All things are possible with God" (Mark 10:27) and "I am with you always" (Matthew 28:20). Wear your belt all day!

THOUGHT OF THE DAY

Can you remember a Bible verse that helps you?

PRAY TODAY

Dear God, thank You for giving me a belt of truth. Help me remember to put it on every day. Amen.

BE GENTLE

Always be gentle with others. The Lord will soon be here.

PHILIPPIANS 4:5 CEV

When you hold a little chick or pet a kitten, you need to use gentle hands so you don't hurt them. When you talk to a baby, you need to use a gentle voice so you don't scare her. But gentleness is important with others too. If you push or pinch someone you might hurt them. If you yell at them or call them names, you might hurt their feelings. God wants us to be good friends. He says we should always be gentle with others. Each person you know is special to God, so treat others with gentleness!

THOUGHT OF THE DAY

Who is gentle with you? Who will you treat gently today?

PRAY TODAY

Dear God, I'm so glad You are gentle with me. Please help me to be gentle with others too. Amen.

DAY 161

YOU CAN ALWAYS COME BACK

Come back to the LORD your God, because he is kind and shows mercy. He doesn't become angry quickly, and he has great love.

JOEL 2:13B NCV

In the Bible, God tells us how to love and care for ourselves and others. When we choose to do what God says, it's like moving even closer to Him. When we don't do what He says, that's called *sin*. And every time we sin, it's as if we move away from God. But guess what? We can always come back.

You come back to God when you tell Him what you did and ask for forgiveness. When you ask, He will forgive you right away! He'll never stop loving you, and He's always ready to welcome you back.

THOUGHT OF THE DAY

God never stops loving you and me.

PRAY TODAY

Dear God, I'm sorry for the times I sinned. Please forgive me, and bring me close to You again! Amen.

DAY 162

SHOWING LOVE

Love is patient and kind, never jealous, boastful, proud, or rude. Love isn't selfish or quick-tempered. It doesn't keep a record of wrongs that others do.

1 CORINTHIANS 13:4–5 CEV

The Bible says that Jesus loves us and that we should love one another. But what does love look like? The apostle Paul wrote a letter to believers to explain what love is. It says: When you are patient, you are showing love. When you don't insist on having your own way or always being first, you are showing love. When you don't get mad over every little thing, you are showing love. When you forgive someone, that's love. These are just a few of the ways you can show love to others! How will you show love today?

THOUGHT OF THE DAY

Showing love is the best way to follow Jesus every day!

PRAY TODAY

Dear God, thank You for showing love to me. Please help me show love to others. Amen.

YOUR GOD STORY

All who worship God, come here and listen; I will tell you everything God has done for me.

PSALM 66:16 CEV

Do you love learning about interesting people? Well guess what? You're one of them!

God made you to be totally unique. And because of that, the way He works in your life is unique too! Does He help you feel confident on your way to school, or calm during arguments? Has He helped you feel better when something sad happened, or brave when you tried something new? Ask God to help you notice His help each day. Those moments make up your very own God Story. And it's a great one!

THOUGHT OF THE DAY

Next time someone asks you about God, just tell your story!

PRAY TODAY

Dear God, please help me notice all the ways You show up every day. Let's write a great story together! Amen.

BE PATIENT AND KIND

Love is patient and kind.

1 CORINTHIANS 13:4A CEV

God knows that we don't always do everything right the first time. But He is patient with us! He forgives us when we make mistakes and He helps us try again. That's because He loves us. In the Bible He reminds us that we should also show love to others by being patient and kind. When you don't get your way, or when lunch isn't ready when you want it, or when a friend doesn't play just the way you wanted, you can show love by being patient and kind. Things always go better when we remember to be patient and kind.

THOUGHT OF THE DAY

Can you think of a time someone was patient and kind to you? How did it feel?

PRAY TODAY

Dear God, I'm so glad You love me. Please help me be patient and kind, just like You. Amen.

BE JOYFUL!

So rejoice in the LORD and be glad, all you who obey him! Shout for joy, all you whose hearts are pure!

PSALM 32:11 NLT

God loves His children to be joyful! All through the Bible there are stories of people who sang songs to God, danced for God, even clapped and shouted for joy to God! When we think about all the amazing things God has done, it makes us glad. When we do what God says, we learn that He knows the best way for us and we're grateful. When we see His creativity in the world He made, we feel amazed. We are God's children, and He loves us. There are so many reasons to rejoice!

THOUGHT OF THE DAY

What are three things that make you joyful today?

PRAY TODAY

Dear God, thank You for loving me so much. Please help me find reasons to be joyful each day. Amen.

DAY 166

SLOW DOWN

To your knowledge, add self-control; and to your self-control, add patience.

2 PETER 1:6 NCV

What would happen if you were in such a hurry to eat your cookies, that you only baked them half as long as the recipe said? Or how good would you be if you tried to play a baseball game after only swinging a bat one time? It takes time to do things the right way, to learn something new, or to get better at a skill. In the Bible, God reminds us that if we want to do something well, it is best to use self-control and be patient. When we slow down, we have time to learn, correct our mistakes, and get better!

THOUGHT OF THE DAY

Slowing down is sometimes the fastest way to do things well!

PRAY TODAY

Dear Lord, thank You for reminding me to slow down. Please help me to be patient when I'm learning new things. Amen.

CHOOSE TO TRUST

Those who know Your name will put their trust in You. For You, O Lord, have never left alone those who look for You.

PSALM 9:10 NLV

Do you know what it means to trust in God? It means to choose to believe what God says about Himself. In the Bible, God says that He loves you. He says that He will never leave you. He says He will help you. He says He will always forgive you. Because God is trustworthy, you can count on Him to do exactly what He says. Sometimes you may not feel like God is there, but trusting God is a choice, not just a feeling. Choose to trust God and He will never let you down.

THOUGHT OF THE DAY

Is it ever hard to trust God?

PRAY TODAY

Dear God, I love You and I'm so glad You love me too. Please help me to choose to trust You every day. Amen.

YOUR SUPERPOWER

"This is my command—be strong and courageous! Do not be afraid or discouraged. For the LORD your God is with you wherever you go."

JOSHUA 1:9 NLT

Superheroes in books and movies often have a special power. Maybe they can fly, or they have a special cape, bracelet, or sword. It is easy to understand why they feel brave! But what about you? Are you sometimes afraid or worried, shy about speaking up or fearful of telling the truth? The Bible says you have the greatest superpower in the universe: "God is with you wherever you go!" When you believe this, you can be brave enough to do the right thing or conquer a hard job. With God, you are strong and courageous!

THOUGHT OF THE DAY

What will you be brave enough to do today?

PRAY TODAY

Dear God, I'm so glad that I can be brave because You are with me wherever I go. Amen.

BE WISE

Wisdom is more precious than rubies. Nothing you could want is equal to it.

PROVERBS 8:11 NCV

A great king named Solomon wrote this Bible verse. He was smart and strong. He had great armies and was very rich. But Solomon knew that none of that mattered if he did not have wisdom. Wisdom is knowing how to use what you have in ways that are right and good. If you have extra time or money, you can use it wisely to help others. If you have toys and books, you can use them wisely by inviting others to play and sharing with them. Ask God for wisdom to use what you have in the best possible way!

THOUGHT OF THE DAY

No matter your size, you can learn to be wise!

PRAY TODAY

Dear God, please help me be wise as I use what You have given me. Amen.

REAL FORGIVENESS

You will throw away all our sins into the deepest part of the sea.

MICAH 7:19B NCV

Sometimes when we've done something wrong and ask for forgiveness, the other person says they will forgive us, but then they keep reminding us of our mistakes. And that makes us feel bad all over again.

God never does that. When we ask God to forgive us, He not only forgives us, but He also gets rid of our sins. The Bible says He throws all those forgiven sins into the deepest part of the ocean! He never reminds us of our mistakes and He loves to give us another chance. God's forgiveness is for real and forever!

THOUGHT OF THE DAY

When you ask God to forgive you, He always does!

PRAY TODAY

Dear God, thank You for giving me real forgiveness that lasts forever. Amen.

NO HIDE AND SEEK

"God did this so that [people] would seek him and perhaps reach out for him and find him, though he is not far from any one of us."

ACTS 17:27 NIV

Have you ever played hide-and-seek? It's a fun game to play with friends, but do you know who won't ever play hide-and-seek with you? God! God wants everyone to find Him, so He never hides from us. He is always near, and we can talk to Him anytime or anywhere. You can talk to God at school or home, on the playground, or in your bed at night. You never have to guess where God is. He loves you so much that He always stays close to you.

THOUGHT OF THE DAY

God will never hide from you.

PRAY TODAY

Dear God, thank You for always staying close to me. I'm so glad You love me. Amen.

DAY 172

GOD ALWAYS HEARS YOU

Be gracious to me, Lord, for I call to You all day long.

PSALM 86:3 HCSB

Do you talk to God before you eat? Do you say prayers at bedtime? Maybe you pray when you're at church or Sunday school. The Bible reminds us that anytime is a great time to talk to God. God is never on vacation or asleep or too busy to hear you. He loves hearing from you any time of the day or night. And there isn't just one way to pray either! You can sing to God, whisper to Him, tell Him about your day, or ask Him questions. He's always happy to hear from you!

THOUGHT OF THE DAY

What's your favorite time to talk to God?

PRAY TODAY

Dear God, I'm glad You're always there to hear me. Thanks for loving me so much. Amen.

A BETTER WAY

For if you refuse to act kindly, you can hardly expect to be treated kindly. Kind mercy wins over harsh judgment every time.

JAMES 2:12–13 MSG

The Bible says we shouldn't be surprised if we do something mean and then someone is mean to us too. Name-calling leads to more name-calling. Hitting leads to more hitting. But the Bible also tells us about a better way. If we are kind even when someone else is mean, we can help stop the meanness and change it to something better. When you are kind, even if it's hard, you are making a choice to follow the example of Jesus. When you refuse to be mean, you are showing others a better way.

THOUGHT OF THE DAY

When unkind words are easy to say, just stop and choose a better way!

PRAY TODAY

Dear God, please help me to choose kind words when I'm tempted to say something mean. Amen.

GOD IS WITH US

"For where two or three are gathered together in My name, I am there among them."

MATTHEW 18:20 HCSB

God lives in the heart of each person who loves Him. That's why He says that whenever we get together with others who love Him, He is with us! It doesn't matter if you are old or young or if there are hundreds of people or just two or three—whenever God's people gather, He is there. He hears your singing and praying. He is there when you read the Bible together and when you care for one another. Remember that whenever you are with others who love and believe in God, He's right there with you!

THOUGHT OF THE DAY

Give thanks to God for being with His people!

PRAY TODAY

Dear God, I'm so glad that You live in me and that You are with Your children whenever we get together. Amen.

FAITH MAKES THINGS POSSIBLE

Jesus replied, "Why do you say 'if you can'? Anything is possible for someone who has faith!"

MARK 9:23 CEV

"Faith" is a Bible word that means believing and trusting that what God says is true. If you believe what Jesus says, you can do anything. You can forgive someone who hurt your feelings because Jesus says forgiving helps both of you. You can share with someone because Jesus says it's important to help others. You can obey your parents because God tells you that's the right choice. You can tell the truth because that's what God wants you to do. All these things are hard, but they are all possible when you have faith.

THOUGHT OF THE DAY

What's something you can do because you have faith in God?

PRAY TODAY

Dear God, please help my faith to grow so that I can do anything You want me to! Amen.

GOD'S BETTER WAY

A man's heart plans his way, but the LORD determines his steps.

PROVERBS 16:9 HCSB

Sometimes we have great ideas, but God's plans are different. That's hard to understand when it happens. Maybe you were really hoping to join the soccer team, but there was no room, so you have to do something else instead. That's disappointing! But if you keep a good attitude, you might find that the new thing is even better! You could meet a great new friend or discover something new you love to do. When your plans don't work out, it's OK to feel upset. But remember to ask God what He's planning. Maybe He's guiding your steps in a better way!

THOUGHT OF THE DAY

Make good plans for every day but pray for God to lead the way!

PRAY TODAY

Dear God, thank You for leading me every day. Please help me keep a good attitude and follow Your way. Amen.

EVERYONE NEEDS FORGIVENESS

Make allowance for each other's faults, and forgive anyone who offends you. Remember, the Lord forgave you, so you must forgive others.

COLOSSIANS 3:13 NLT

Is it ever hard to forgive someone? If you're angry or hurt, it can feel impossible! So the Bible reminds you of something that can help: you've needed forgiveness too.

The next time someone makes you angry, try to remember a time when you made a mistake. Nobody's perfect! That doesn't mean that what happened is OK. But remembering when you've messed up can help you understand that person a little better and maybe feel a little less angry. Talk about how you're feeling. Then ask God to help you forgive. He forgives each of us over and over, so we can do it too!

THOUGHT OF THE DAY

Understanding how someone feels is called empathy.

PRAY TODAY

Dear God, when I get angry, help me remember how many times You've forgiven me. Then help me give that gift to others. Amen.

THE WISDOM OF TRUTH

You want me to be completely truthful, so teach me wisdom.

PSALM 51:6 NCV

Do you ever feel like lying is easier than telling the truth? Sometimes it seems that way. But God says the truth is always the wise choice.

When you tell a lie, you might get what you want right away. But you'll probably have to make up more lies to keep the truth a secret! You might feel sad or scared inside. You might even end up hurting someone else. But with the truth, there's none of those bad feelings! So instead, ask God to give you the wisdom and courage to tell the truth. The truth pleases God, and it's best for everyone!

THOUGHT OF THE DAY

When others know you say what's true, they'll want to be good friends with you!

PRAY TODAY

Dear God, sometimes I'm tempted to lie. Help me to be wise and brave every day, so I will always choose the truth. Amen.

DAY 179

HELPFUL WORDS

LORD, help me control my tongue; help me be careful about what I say.

PSALM 141:3 NCV

There is a small part of your body that is very powerful. It is also hard to control. Can you guess what it is? It's your tongue!

Your tongue is so powerful because you use it to talk. And the words that come out of your mouth have the power to help people or to hurt them. Has someone ever said words that hurt your feelings? Have you ever said words that hurt someone else? We need God's help to make sure our words don't hurt others. Be sure to ask Him to help you control your tongue each day!

THOUGHT OF THE DAY

How will you use your words to help someone today?

PRAY TODAY

Dear God, please help me remember that my words are important. Please help me to always use words that help. Amen.

BEING PATIENT

Always be humble and gentle. Be patient and accept each other with love.

EPHESIANS 4:2 ICB

Are you ever impatient? It's hard to wait for things you want. It's hard to not be able to do something the first time you try. It's hard to take turns. Patience is a way of showing others and ourselves that we don't always have to have our way.

When we let someone else go first, we are being patient. We are also being patient when we don't whine while waiting or when we give someone time to think.

Being patient isn't always easy, but God says that when we are patient, we are showing love.

THOUGHT OF THE DAY

When have you been patient? What are some ways you can show patience?

PRAY TODAY

Dear God, thank You for always being patient with me. Please help me be patient with other people too. Amen.

GOD'S LOVE LASTS

You are my God, and I will praise you; you are my God, and I will exalt you. Give thanks to the LORD, for he is good; his love endures forever.

PSALM 118:28–29 NIV

Sometimes we get rid of things because they wear out, get old, or break. As you get bigger, you grow out of your clothes and even certain toys. But do you know what never changes? God's love for you!

God's love never wears out, gets old, or breaks. And you will never outgrow it! The Bible says, "His love endures forever." You can be sure that God's love for you will always be there. You can't do anything to lose it. So be sure to thank Him for His wonderful love that never changes.

THOUGHT OF THE DAY

God's love is forever!

PRAY TODAY

Dear God, thank You for always loving me and for never leaving me. Amen.

DAY 182

TRUTH TAKES PRACTICE

We are part of the same body. Stop lying and start telling each other the truth.

EPHESIANS 4:25 CEV

Is it ever hard to tell the truth? You're not alone! Even people in the Bible had trouble with lying sometimes. But God says that being honest is always the best choice—even when we don't feel like it.

So how do you get better at doing something hard? Just practice! Tell the truth about small things, so you'll be ready when big things come along. And if you've already told a lie? It's not too late! Tell the person what happened and see if you can help make things right. As you practice more and more, the truth will become much easier than lying!

THOUGHT OF THE DAY

Practice telling the truth until it becomes a habit.

PRAY TODAY

Dear God, sometimes it's so hard to tell the truth. Will You please help me practice whenever I can? Amen.

STRENGTH FROM GOD

We say they are happy because they did not give up.

JAMES 5:11A NCV

It's amazing to see star athletes, musicians, and artists do what they do. But they weren't always that way—everybody starts as beginners! They worked hard to get so good, and most of them still work hard to stay that way.

Beginning something can be hard . . . and sometimes boring. But if you want to get better at anything, you can't give up! God can help. When you feel frustrated, ask God for strength to try again. If you get bored, ask God to help you find fun in each step. When you don't give up, you get better every day!

THOUGHT OF THE DAY

God is always with you, so you'll always have help!

PRAY TODAY

Dear God, thank You for helping me when things get hard. Help me never to give up on things that matter! Amen.

BETTER THAN ONE

Two people are better off than one, for they can help each other succeed. If one person falls, the other can reach out and help. But someone who falls alone is in real trouble.

ECCLESIASTES 4:9–10 NLT

Even if you're someone who likes to do things by yourself, sometimes it's nice to spend time with other people. Stuck on an art project? A friend can help you think up new ideas! Bored of playing by yourself? Invite your younger sibling to play with you! And do you ever have feelings that are confusing? Sharing with a parent or a teacher you trust can help you work through a problem or at least feel a little better. God has put people in your life to build you up and help you grow!

THOUGHT OF THE DAY

Who is someone you like spending time with?

PRAY TODAY

Dear God, please help me enjoy my alone time and work well with others too! Amen.

DO YOU LOOK LIKE GOD?

So God created human beings in his own image.

GENESIS 1:27A NLT

Have you ever noticed that some people look alike? Brothers and sisters sometimes look similar; good friends might even dress the same after a while!

God made each of us in His image—that means we all look a little like Him on the inside. How cool is that?! Each of us can imagine how others feel and choose to put their needs above our own. We can create and imagine new things. We can love and be loved. And each time we choose to do these things, others will see God in us a little more clearly.

THOUGHT OF THE DAY

Who do you think you look like? What's a way you can "look" more like God?

PRAY TODAY

Dear God, I'm so proud to be in Your family. Help me look more like You each day. Amen.

DAY 186

SHOW YOUR LOVE

There are three things that remain—faith, hope, and love—and the greatest of these is love.

1 CORINTHIANS 13:13 TLB

We often use the word "love" to say how we feel about something: "I love pizza!" or "I love my family." But when the Bible talks about love, it reminds us that love is more than a feeling. It's a way of acting. The Bible says love is patient, kind, loyal, not jealous, not bragging, not proud, not selfish or rude, and forgiving of others.

So real love, God's kind of love, is something we do. Every day you can look for ways to show love to your friends and family. Give it a try! Be creative about how you show love to others.

THOUGHT OF THE DAY

Can you name some ways others have shown their love to you? How can you show your love to someone else?

PRAY TODAY

Dear God, I want to show Your love to others. Will You help me find ways to do this every day? Amen.

TOUGH FORGIVENESS

Never pay back evil with more evil. Do things in such a way that everyone can see that you are honorable.

ROMANS 12:17 NLT

Forgiveness isn't always easy. When someone hurts you, you may want to hurt them back! But God tells us to forgive, even when it's hard.

The Bible tells a story of two brothers named Jacob and Esau. Jacob stole from Esau, and then ran away from home! When Jacob came back years later, he was scared that Esau would hurt him. But Esau had forgiven Jacob long ago! He ran out to greet his brother with hugs and kisses and celebration. Because Esau chose forgiveness, Jacob was safe, and Esau had joy in his life. Forgiveness is good for everyone!

THOUGHT OF THE DAY

Do you feel angry toward someone? Ask God to help you forgive them!

PRAY TODAY

Dear God, I don't want to stay angry. Please teach me how to forgive so I can feel better and help others too. Amen.

USE KIND WORDS

A kind answer soothes angry feelings, but harsh words stir them up.

PROVERBS 15:1 CEV

We all get angry. Maybe our feelings were hurt, or someone pushed ahead of us in line. Maybe we wanted to have something and our parents said "No." You can't help feeling angry, but you can help what you say when you're mad or upset.

If we use angry words, we just make things worse. It's like stirring up a fire. But, if we use kind words and don't yell or scream, it calms down the angry feelings. It isn't easy, but things go so much better if we remember to use kind words instead of angry ones.

THOUGHT OF THE DAY

Choose some kind words you can say next time you're feeling upset. It helps to have a plan!

PRAY TODAY

Dear God, please help me to use kind words instead of mean ones when I feel angry. Amen.

DAY 189

GOD'S ON YOUR SIDE

Now the God of all grace, who called you to His eternal glory in Christ Jesus, will personally restore, establish, strengthen, and support you . . .

1 PETER 5:10 HCSB

Do you ever feel frustrated? Or just lonely or confused? There's Someone special who is always cheering you on. Whether you are feeling sad or glad or even if you're feeling mad, God is right beside you. He loves you and wants to help you, no matter what's going on. Nothing worries God and nothing is too hard for Him.

Next time you feel like you need a little help, talk to God about it. He's on your side and He wants to help you. He will give you strength to do hard things and patience to get through tough times.

THOUGHT OF THE DAY

With God on your side, you can face anything!

PRAY TODAY

Dear God, thanks for always being on my side. Please help me to remember to talk to You whenever I need help. Amen.

WHO'S FIRST?

Don't be selfish. . . . Be humble, thinking of others as better than yourself.

PHILIPPIANS 2:3 TLB

Do you like being the line leader or being chosen first on a team? It feels special to be first, but the Bible shows us a way to be even more special. It's called being humble. When we are humble, we let others go first. That's what Jesus did!

Jesus was God's Son, and that made Him the most special person who ever lived. But He knew that putting others first showed them how special they were to God. What an amazing gift to give! It isn't always easy to let others go first, but it's a great way to be more like Jesus!

THOUGHT OF THE DAY

What are some ways you can show others they are special?

PRAY TODAY

Dear God, please help me to put others first even when it isn't easy. Help me be more like You. Amen.

DAY 191

LOOK FOR GOODNESS

The one who searches for what is good finds favor, but if someone looks for trouble, it will come to him.

PROVERBS 11:27 HCSB

If you want to find something, what do you do? You look for it!

Do you want to find good things? They are everywhere! Look for goodness in everyone you meet. Notice the beautiful songs that birds sing or the delicious smell of dinner cooking. Search for something happy in everything that happens. Even bad days have some good hidden in them.

If you spend your time focusing on things that make you sad or angry, that's all you'll see. Instead, look for good! God can help you find exactly what you need.

THOUGHT OF THE DAY

What are three good things that happened today?

PRAY TODAY

Dear God, You made such a good world! Please help me look for goodness all day every day! Amen.

DAY 192

NEVER GIVE UP

We can rejoice, too, when we run into problems and trials, for we know that they are good for us—they help us learn to be patient. And patience develops strength of character in us and helps us trust God more each time we use it until finally our hope and faith are strong and steady.

ROMANS 5:3–4 TLB

Sometimes when things are hard to do, we might feel like giving up. But if we quit, we won't learn how to do them. If you gave up trying you might never learn to do important things like write your name or count or make friends. The Bible says it is good to keep trying when things are hard because that helps us grow. Remember, you're not in this alone. God will always help us learn new things if we don't give up!

THOUGHT OF THE DAY

Trying hard is the thing to do when you're learning something new!

PRAY TODAY

Dear God, thank You for helping me to grow. Please help me to keep trying even when things are hard to do. Amen.

PICK JESUS

"Follow Me," Jesus told them, "and I will make you fish for people!" Immediately they left their nets and followed Him.

MARK 1:17–18 HCSB

Who are some good leaders in your life? Do you have a teacher who explains things well? Maybe your parents help you make smart choices when you're feeling confused. When you choose to follow a good leader, you'll never get lost!

Jesus is the best leader of all. When we follow Him, we learn to be kind and brave. He shows us the best ways to help others, and guides us through difficult times. And He will lead you to amazing blessings! Jesus knows the way to your very best life. So stay close to Him!

THOUGHT OF THE DAY

Jesus knows the way; just follow Him each day!

PRAY TODAY

Dear Jesus, please help me choose to follow You every day. You always lead me to good things! Amen.

THE GIFT OF FORGIVENESS

"I will forgive their wrongdoing, and I will never again remember their sins."

HEBREWS 8:12 CSB

One of God's best gifts is forgiveness! And we can have it any time we need it.

We all have rules we need to follow. And when you break the rules, it doesn't feel great, does it? If you keep it a secret, you might feel yucky inside. If you hurt someone else, it might make you feel sad. You might even get in trouble. But God will always forgive you. All you have to do is ask! Then, He can fill you with courage to make things right, and to do better next time. His love is bigger than any mistakes we make!

THOUGHT OF THE DAY

God forgives you right away. The gift is free, so ask today!

PRAY TODAY

Dear God, thank You for the awesome gift of forgiveness. Please help me talk to You right away when I make mistakes. Amen.

MAKING MISTAKES

"You're blessed when you're content with just who you are—no more, no less."

MATTHEW 5:5 MSG

God made you. He loves you, and He has great plans for you. He wants you to become the person He created you to be. But that doesn't mean you will never make mistakes. In fact, making mistakes is just another way to grow.

When you are learning to kick a ball or draw a picture, to ride a bike or read a book, you won't always get it right. That is perfectly OK! If you keep on trying, you will get better. Be happy that you are growing and learning. That's just how God planned it!

THOUGHT OF THE DAY

Can you name three things that you are learning to do?

PRAY TODAY

Dear God, I'm glad You made me and that You love me. Help me keep trying, even when I make mistakes. Amen.

BEING FRIENDS

Be kind to each other, tenderhearted, forgiving one another, just as God through Christ has forgiven you.

EPHESIANS 4:32 NLT

The Bible tells us that friendship is very important. Jesus even calls His followers His friends! But if we want to have good friends, we have to be willing to be a good friend.

Friends are kind and take care of one another. Friends forgive when they make mistakes. Friends tell each other the truth. If you look for ways to treat others the way you would like to be treated, you will always have good friends. And you'll be a good friend too!

THOUGHT OF THE DAY

Can you name some of your good friends? What is it that makes them such good friends?

PRAY TODAY

Dear God, I am so glad You have given me good friends. Will You please help me to be a good friend too? Amen.

THE ONE AND ONLY YOU!

For you created my inmost being; you knit me together in my mother's womb. I praise you because I am fearfully and wonderfully made.

PSALM 139:13–14 NIV

God worked really hard to make you. He gave you a smile that only you have. He made your eyes and ears and nose unique. He chose your hair color and decided where to put each freckle—or maybe decided you wouldn't have freckles at all! God lovingly designed you to be exactly the way you are. There is only one you!

So don't believe anyone who says you should look or act or sound a certain way. The world needs you just how you are. That's why God made you that way!

THOUGHT OF THE DAY

What's something special about you?

PRAY TODAY

Dear God, thank You for all the ways You made me special. I love being Your child! Amen.

BE A BLESSING

"It is more blessed to give than to receive."

ACTS 20:35B ESV

The word "blessed" means to be happy. Jesus says we will be happier giving to others than just getting things for ourselves. When you take time to think about what will make someone else happy, you will feel happier too!

You may not have money to spend on fancy gifts, but you can always give a hug, share a smile, lend a toy to a friend, draw a picture, or make a card. As you think about giving something to others, you will start to feel happy, and probably even excited! Be a blessing, and you will be blessed!

THOUGHT OF THE DAY

What is one way you can be a blessing to someone in your family?

PRAY TODAY

Dear God, thank You for all You give to me every single day. Please help me find ways to be a blessing to others. Amen.

GOD'S CURE FOR SIN

But if we confess our sins to God, he can always be trusted to forgive us and take our sins away.

1 JOHN 1:9 CEV

Sin is when we do things our way instead of God's way. Everyone in the world sins because we all want things our own way. But sin doesn't make us happy for very long, and it doesn't make God happy either. That's because sin pulls us away from God and from other people too.

Since God loves us, He wants us to be close to Him. God says that if we will tell Him about our sins and ask Him to forgive us, He will! When God takes our sins away, we feel close to God again and closer to others too.

THOUGHT OF THE DAY

Telling God about our sin lets God's forgiveness come right in!

PRAY TODAY

Dear God, thank You for Your loving forgiveness that cures my sin. Help me to live like You want me to. Amen.

DAY 200

JESUS LOVES YOU NO MATTER WHAT

But God showed how much he loved us by having Christ die for us, even though we were sinful.

ROMANS 5:8 CEV

Do you think you have to do everything right? Are you afraid of trying something new because you might make a mistake? The Bible says that Jesus loves you no matter what. So you can be brave! You can try new things without worrying about making mistakes, because you can never lose God's love.

Jesus loves you so much that He gave up His life so you could live with Him forever. He knows you and He cares for you—even when you make mistakes. He wants to help you and He will never leave you.

THOUGHT OF THE DAY

How does Jesus' love help you to be brave?

PRAY TODAY

Dear God, thank You for loving me so much. Please help me to trust in Your love every day. Amen.

DAY 201

SHARING BRINGS JOY

Do not neglect to do good and to share what you have, for such sacrifices are pleasing to God.

HEBREWS 13:16 ESV

God has given you many wonderful things—a smile, great ideas, books, toys, adventures, flowers, and lots more! Do you know why God gives His children so much? It's so that we have things to share with each other.

God made us, so He knows that we are happiest when we give some of what we have to other people. You can share a smile with a sad friend, read a story to someone, sing a song, paint a picture, or share a toy. When you share, you make God happy, and you are happier too! That's real joy.

THOUGHT OF THE DAY

Think about something you can share with someone . . . then do it!

PRAY TODAY

Dear God, thank You for giving me so much. Help me bring joy to others by sharing what I have with them. Amen.

BRING THE LIGHT

The light shines in the darkness, and the darkness has not overcome it.

JOHN 1:5 ESV

When you go into a dark room and turn on the light, what happens? The darkness goes away! When the sun comes up, what happens to the dark night? It goes away!

When Jesus lives in you, you are like a light, shining in the darkness. How does that work? If someone is sad, and you offer them kindness, you're sharing the light of Jesus. If someone tells a lie, and you say what is true, your words help everyone see what's right. When you belong to Jesus, you carry His light wherever you go. And God's light always chases away the darkness.

THOUGHT OF THE DAY

How can you bring Jesus' light to someone today?

PRAY TODAY

Dear God, help me look for ways to bring Your light to others today. Amen.

DAY 203

DO SOMETHING BIG!

You are young, but do not let anyone treat you as if you were not important. Be an example to show the believers how they should live. Show them with your words, with the way you live, with your love, with your faith, and with your pure life.

1 TIMOTHY 4:12 ICB

Has someone ever told you that you're too little to do something? That's frustrating, isn't it? But even though there are some things only grown-ups or older kids can do, you can do some really big things too! When you invite a new friend to play, you help him or her feel loved and important. When you share what you have, you show God's love. And when you pray, you're talking to the King of the whole universe! The things you do matter big-time to God.

THOUGHT OF THE DAY

With God's help, little people can do great big things!

PRAY TODAY

Dear God, sometimes it's hard to be little. Please show me what kinds of big things I can do for You! Amen.

LET'S GET ALONG!

Work at getting along with each other and with God.

HEBREWS 12:14 MSG

It's easy to get along with people who are just like us. But the world is full of people who think and act differently from us. God wants us to work hard to get along with everyone—not just the people we already like.

Start by showing kindness to everyone you meet. Get to know people who are different from you. You probably won't become best friends with each person. And there may be things you disagree about. That's OK! Getting along means appreciating what makes each other special. Then, you can all work together to learn, grow, and do big things.

THOUGHT OF THE DAY

Is there someone who is hard to get along with? How can you show kindness to that person?

PRAY TODAY

Dear God, thank You for making all kinds of people. Help me get along with those who are different from me! Amen.

TRUE FRIENDS

A friend loves you all the time.

PROVERBS 17:17 ICB

What do you and your friends like to do together? Do you make each other laugh? Do you have favorite games? It's important to have fun together, of course! But God says a true friend sticks around even if things aren't always fun.

When your friends have a bad day, make sure they know that you still love them. If you get into an argument, be willing to listen and say "sorry" when you need to. And remember that your friends should love you on your bad days too. When you find true friends, hang on to them!

THOUGHT OF THE DAY

True friends are true gifts from God!

PRAY TODAY

Dear God, thank You for the gift of friends. Please help me find—and be!—a true friend. Amen.

OBEY EACH DAY

But Jesus said, "Those who hear the teaching of God and obey it—they are the ones who are truly blessed."

LUKE 11:28 ICB

Moses was a great leader. But he wasn't always that way. One day, while Moses was tending sheep, God told him to go and challenge a powerful king. Moses was surprised and scared! He didn't like to talk in front of people, and he knew the king was dangerous. But God promised He would help Moses, so Moses obeyed. And because of that, Moses did great things!

God has a plan for your life too! When you pray, ask God to show you what to do each day. When you obey God like Moses did, you can do great things!

THOUGHT OF THE DAY

Sometimes God's ideas are surprising, like loving your enemies! Can you do that?

PRAY TODAY

Dear God, please help me obey You, even when You tell me to do something scary or surprising! Amen.

FIND WHAT'S GOOD

A happy heart makes the face cheerful, but heartache crushes the spirit.

PROVERBS 15:13 NIV

Some days you just feel grumpy. Here's a game to help your heart feel happy again.

Every time something makes you grumpy, see if you can find something good too. Are you out of your favorite breakfast food? Make something wacky for breakfast instead. Is your friend playing with someone else at recess? Find someone new to play with! Does a rainstorm mean you can't play baseball today? Maybe, but it also means you can play hide-and-seek inside! Spend your time looking for good things, and you'll cheer up your grumpy heart in no time!

THOUGHT OF THE DAY

Look for good things in the bad. Soon you might not feel so sad!

PRAY TODAY

Dear God, when I feel down, please help me find good things to cheer up my heart. Amen.

DAY 208

CALL THE DOCTOR!

A cheerful heart is good medicine, but a broken spirit saps a person's strength.

PROVERBS 17:22 NLT

You probably know that you feel better when you're cheerful. But did you know that you can share your cheer to help others feel better too? You'll be like a happiness doctor!

Share a hug or a high five with a good friend. Wave to your neighbors when they walk by your house. Invite a new friend to play your favorite game at recess. Tell jokes around the dinner table and see who laughs the hardest!

When you have a cheerful heart, share it with the world.

THOUGHT OF THE DAY

Surprise someone who is sad with super silly smiles!

PRAY TODAY

Dear God, I love feeling cheerful! Help me share my smiles with everyone around me! Amen.

THE ONLY YOU

I will praise You because I have been remarkably and wonderfully made. Your works are wonderful, and I know this very well.

PSALM 139:14 HCSB

Do you have a friend who can run super fast? Or a sibling who can draw anything? Or a classmate who always seems to get the right answer? It's tempting to compare yourself with others, especially when they can do something you'd like to do. But God never does that. He made everyone with a unique purpose. That means there is only one you!

If you feel discouraged, remember how much God loves you. Then pray for Him to show you what strengths He's given you. You aren't supposed to be like everyone else. We already have them—the world needs YOU!

THOUGHT OF THE DAY

What are you good at?

PRAY TODAY

Dear God, thank You for making me just the way I am. Please show me how to be the best me! Amen.

BEING THANKFUL

I said to myself, "Relax and rest. God has showered you with blessings."

PSALM 116:7 MSG

You probably know it's polite to say "thank you" when you get a birthday gift. But you get all sorts of gifts every single day! Your parents give you love, a home, good food, and many other things. Do you remember to say "thank you" to them?

And don't forget about God! When you look at the world around you, try to notice all the amazing things that God has given you. Birds, rainbows, puffy white clouds, shady trees, warm sunshine, and oceans are just a few of His blessings. So remember to thank God each day too!

THOUGHT OF THE DAY

Can you name five blessings God has given you?

PRAY TODAY

Dear God, You are so amazing. I just want to thank You for everything You have given to me! Amen.

A SPECIAL UNIFORM

So, chosen by God for this new life of love, dress in the wardrobe God picked out for you: compassion, kindness, humility, quiet strength, discipline.

COLOSSIANS 3:12 MSG

Some people wear uniforms that help them do their jobs well. Firefighters' special suits keep them safe in burning buildings. Soccer players wear matching jerseys so they can easily spot their teammates. Men and women in the military wear uniforms that tell people about the work they do.

You have important work to do for God. So be sure you're dressed for it! Think about kindness and humility like a jacket you put on every day, or self-control like a favorite hat. Don't leave home without God's special uniform!

THOUGHT OF THE DAY

Dress up in the love of God!

PRAY TODAY

Dear God, when I get up each morning, please help me remember to put on kindness, strength, and self-control too. Amen.

DAY 212

LOVE CAN HELP

Hatred stirs up trouble, but love forgives all wrongs.

PROVERBS 10:12 NCV

When someone makes you mad, you might want to stay angry—or even hurt them back! But God tells us to forgive instead.

But how do you do that? The secret is love. Even if you don't feel love for that person yet (it's hard when you're hurt!), look for ways to act lovingly toward them. One way you can do that is to pray for the person who hurt you. Then pick one nice thing to say to them. Choosing not to say unkind words is a loving choice too! The more you practice love, the easier it will be to forgive—this time and every time!

THOUGHT OF THE DAY

How will you choose love next time someone upsets you?

PRAY TODAY

Dear God, will You please help me be loving and forgiving? It sounds a lot better than staying mad. Amen.

GROWING IN GOD

But grow in the grace and knowledge of our Lord and Savior Jesus Christ. To Him be the glory both now and forever. Amen.

2 PETER 3:18 NKJV

Your body grows bigger and stronger each day. But you can grow in another important way too: You can grow in God!

You grow in your knowledge of God when you read Bible stories and ask good questions. You grow in God's grace when you make choices that show you trust Him. That can mean inviting someone new to play, giving away some of your allowance to help others, or praying when you feel afraid. What's your favorite way to "grow in God"?

THOUGHT OF THE DAY

When you grow strong in God, you can do great things!

PRAY TODAY

Dear God, please help me learn more about You and to trust You more each day. Amen.

COUNT YOUR BLESSINGS

You are wonderful . . . you store up blessings for all who honor and trust you.

PSALM 31:19 CEV

There is an old song that says when you count your blessings, you'll see all that God has done. It's important to remember that every good thing you have is a blessing or gift from God. Blessings can be small like a tiny flower, or huge like the ocean. They can be close, like your family, or far away, like the stars and moon. When you take time to name the good things God has given you, it makes you realize how much He loves you. And it makes you thankful too!

THOUGHT OF THE DAY

How many blessings can you count in one minute?

PRAY TODAY

Dear God, You have given me so many wonderful blessings. Please help me remember to always be thankful to You! Amen.

BE A HELPER

Don't get tired of helping others. You will be rewarded when the time is right, if you don't give up.

GALATIANS 6:9 CEV

Doesn't it make you happy when you have a job to do and a friend offers to help? Maybe you have to walk the dog and your sister comes with you. Maybe you're trying to learn something new, and your buddy helps you practice. When a friend gives you a hand, things are more fun and the work goes faster. So be sure you find ways to help others too! Everyone can use a helping hand and God even promises to bless us when we take time to help others!

THOUGHT OF THE DAY

Who has helped you recently? Who can you help today?

PRAY TODAY

Dear God, thank You for always helping me. Please show me how I can help someone today. Amen.

DAY 216

SHOW SOME RESPECT

Show respect for all people.

1 PETER 2:17A ICB

Each person in the world is created and loved by God. That's why He tells us in the Bible to "show respect for all people." We show respect when we listen patiently, when we take turns, and when we are kind. We speak with respect when we say "please," "thanks," and "I'm sorry." It is easy to show respect to our best friends, but the Bible says we should show respect for everyone. Practice treating everyone with respect, the way you would like them to treat you, and it will become easier every day.

THOUGHT OF THE DAY

Why do you think God wants us to be respectful to everyone, not just people we like?

PRAY TODAY

Dear God, thank You for creating and loving each person in the world. Help me to show respect to everyone I meet. Amen.

DAY 217

TIME WITH GOD

"But when you pray, go into your private room, shut your door, and pray to your Father who is in secret."

MATTHEW 6:6A HCSB

What does your usual day look like? Maybe you have a special way you get ready for school in the morning. Maybe you have story time before bed. To make your day the best it can be, set aside some time with God too!

Jesus said the best way to spend time with God is to pray. Talk to Him just like you would talk to a best friend! Ask Him your questions and tell Him your ideas. Talk about what's worrying you. Share a funny story! God loves to hear from you. So find a special place and spend some time with Him each day.

THOUGHT OF THE DAY

To have the best talks with God, find a place without a lot of distractions!

PRAY TODAY

Dear God, I want to be better friends with You. Please help me make time every day so we can talk together! Amen.

TALKING TO GOD

I cried to him for help; I praised him with songs.

PSALM 66:17 GNT

Do you have a good friend you love talking to? Friends share joys and even sadness with each other. God is a friend who wants to hear all about what is going on in your life too!

Talking to God is called prayer. And you can pray anytime you want to. God is always around! You can tell Him when you're feeling sad or even mad. You can talk about happy times and scary times. When you pray, you can whisper or shout or even sing! God loves to hear your voice.

THOUGHT OF THE DAY

What are some things you want to tell God about right now?

PRAY TODAY

Dear God, thank You for being my best friend. Help me to remember to talk with You every day. Amen.

POWERFUL KINDNESS

"Do what is right and true. Be kind and merciful to each other."

ZECHARIAH 7:9B NCV

Zechariah was a man who told people about God. One day, the people asked Zechariah what God wanted them to do. Do you know the only thing God asked for? Kindness.

That's because kindness is super powerful! Think about everything kindness can do. It can encourage a frustrated friend. It can comfort a sad neighbor. When you choose kind words, you can stop someone's anger or heal someone's embarrassment. With kindness and patience, you can even teach others new things. If anyone wants you to act in unkind ways, don't fall for it! God knows that caring for others is the most powerful choice of all!

THOUGHT OF THE DAY

Kindness comes in lots of forms: patience and generosity are good places to start!

PRAY TODAY

Dear God, I want to be powerful! Please help me choose kindness every day. Amen.

DAY 220

GOOD FRUIT

But the fruit of the Spirit is love, joy, peace, patience, kindness, goodness, faithfulness, gentleness, self-control; against such things there is no law.

GALATIANS 5:22–23 ESV

Do you know how fruit grows in a garden? Every delicious strawberry or bright tomato comes from a tiny seed, planted in good soil and watered often. The Bible says you are like a seed in a garden, and God is the rich soil and fresh water you need. When you follow Him, you will grow strong and produce wonderful things.

Maybe joy and peace will sprout at unexpected times! Or gentleness will bloom, even when you feel angry. Or self-control will ripen right when you need it! So spend time with God by praying and reading the Bible. Think of it as watering your garden!

THOUGHT OF THE DAY

Reread today's verse. What fruit do you want to grow in your heart?

PRAY TODAY

Dear God, please help me follow You closely so that I can grow good fruit! Amen.

INSIDE OR OUTSIDE

"God does not see the same way people see. People look at the outside of a person, but the LORD looks at the heart."

1 SAMUEL 16:7B NCV

David was the youngest and smallest kid in his family. But God still chose him to be king! That's because David loved God with his whole heart.

Do you ever worry about what you look like? Guess what? God doesn't! He looks right past the outside to what's inside you! He sees your heart, and that's all that matters to Him. And that's how He wants us to see others too. So don't worry about the way you look or the clothes you wear. When your heart loves God and cares for others, you're beautiful!

THOUGHT OF THE DAY

Try to see others the way God sees you—heart first!

PRAY TODAY

Dear God, thank You for loving me just the way I am. Please give me a heart that makes You happy! Amen.

SHARE A SMILE

Happiness makes a person smile, but sadness can break a person's spirit.

PROVERBS 15:13 NCV

How do you feel when you see someone smiling? Does it make you feel happy too? Maybe you want to check out what's making them cheerful! Maybe you feel warm inside because that smile means they're happy to see you. When you're feeling sad, just seeing someone smile can help you feel better.

You can share your smile too. Try it out! When you see a friend or someone you know, try smiling at them first and see how many friends you can get to smile back. Pretty soon, you'll be an expert at spreading happiness.

THOUGHT OF THE DAY

Smiles are the easiest things to share. There are always enough to go around!

PRAY TODAY

Dear God, I'm glad I can share happiness with others. Thank You for the gift of smiles! Amen.

SINGING TO GOD

It is good to praise the LORD and make music to your name, O Most High.

PSALM 92:1 NIV

The world is filled with many different kinds of music. In the city you might hear the rumble of cars, the chimes of a church bell, or the high wail of a fire truck. At the ocean you might hear the roaring waves and the water swishing on the sand. In the woods you might hear birds chirping or frogs croaking.

There are sounds all around you, but the Bible says God especially loves to hear His children making music and singing songs to Him. What kinds of songs can you sing to tell God how much you love Him?

THOUGHT OF THE DAY

What is your favorite kind of music?

PRAY TODAY

Dear God, thank You for giving me a voice so I can sing praises to You! Amen.

DAY 224

WHAT MAKES YOU HAPPY?

I will be happy because of you; God Most High, I will sing praises to your name.

PSALM 9:2 NCV

What makes you happy? Is it getting a new toy or winning a game? These are fun things, but when our happiness depends on what we get, it can quickly disappear when things don't go our way.

The Bible shows us a better way to be happy. We can be happy because of God! Just think about the wonderful things God gives you: God's love lasts forever. He always cares for you, and He will never leave you. Thinking about these things will help you be happy . . . even when you don't get everything you want!

THOUGHT OF THE DAY

Name something God has given you that makes you happy!

PRAY TODAY

Dear God, thinking about how much You love me makes me happy! Thank You! Amen.

HOW GOD LOVES

This is what real love is: It is not our love for God; it is God's love for us. He sent his Son to die in our place to take away our sins.

1 JOHN 4:10 NCV

God's love is not just an idea. It is something He does for us. God knows that we don't always do what's right. He knows we need to be forgiven. So God sent Jesus to live a perfect life. Then Jesus died on the cross to pay the price for the wrong things we do, so we can be forgiven and live with Him forever.

God loved you before you were born. He cares about you now and will always love you. When you love and forgive others, you show God how much you love Him back.

THOUGHT OF THE DAY

God loves you and now you know it! Share His love by how you show it!

PRAY TODAY

Dear God, thank You for sending Jesus so I can be forgiven and know Your love. Please help me share Your love with others. Amen.

WHAT'S IT FOR?

Every part of Scripture is God-breathed and useful one way or another.

2 TIMOTHY 3:16A MSG

The Bible is full of great stories. Some are exciting and some are peaceful. Some are short and some are long—some are even told in poems! And God has something to teach us in each one.

The story of Joseph and his brothers in Genesis teaches us to be faithful and trust God. The story of Jesus meeting a woman at the well helps us understand God's love for all people. When you hear Bible stories, try to figure out what God wants you to learn. Every verse is there for a reason!

THOUGHT OF THE DAY

Who's your favorite Bible character? What's God teaching you through him or her?

PRAY TODAY

Dear God, I love to hear Bible stories. Help me listen closely so I can learn the things You want me to! Amen.

DAY 227

WORK CHEERFULLY

Work hard and cheerfully at all you do.

COLOSSIANS 3:23A TLB

When you think of chores, do you feel cheerful? That might seem like a silly question! But God tells us to work hard AND to work cheerfully. So can you find ways to enjoy the work you have to do?

Maybe you can make up a game for getting all your chores finished. Or try making up a funny song like Larry does to help you study for school! Clean up your toys with a friend and race to see who can finish first. Surprise your mom and dad by doing stuff without being asked! When you have fun with your work, you'll do an even better job!

THOUGHT OF THE DAY

God loves a happy worker.

PRAY TODAY

Dear God, please show me how I can work cheerfully and do all my work well! Amen.

WAITING PATIENTLY

I waited patiently for the LORD. He turned to me and heard my cry.

PSALM 40:1 NCV

God has good plans for you. He knows your dreams, and He wants to give you good things. He also knows the perfect time to give you everything you need. But it can be hard to wait for God's timing!

The Bible says to wait patiently for God. Patience means you trust God to do what He's promised. It means waiting with hope and excitement about what He has in store for you. Talk to God often. Ask Him to show you the best way to live each day. Share your ideas with Him. Then watch and see what He does! He won't let you down.

THOUGHT OF THE DAY

God hears every prayer. He's working on big plans for you!

PRAY TODAY

Dear God, thank You for hearing my prayers! Help me to trust You and wait patiently, even when it's hard. Amen.

PEACE ON THE INSIDE

Only God gives inward peace, and I depend on him.

PSALM 62:5 CEV

Have you ever wished you could change what's happening around you? Sometimes, things happen that we can't control. But God has a great gift for you: inward peace. Inward peace is when God helps you feel calm inside no matter what.

When you have peace on the inside, you can handle anything. If you're scared of the dark, God can help you feel less afraid. If school gets frustrating, God can help you slow down and find a solution. So don't worry if you have tough days or sad times. God's inward peace will help you through it all!

THOUGHT OF THE DAY

When you can't change what's outside, God can change what's inside!

PRAY TODAY

Dear God, I'm so glad You give me peace on the inside. It's one more way I know You're always with me. Amen.

THE TRUTH IS KIND

Since you put away lying, Speak the truth, each one to his neighbor, because we are members of one another.

EPHESIANS 4:25 HCSB

Have you ever felt like telling a lie? Sometimes it's hard to tell the truth! But God says that we should always be honest. That's because honesty is kind. Truthful people play fair, admit when they are wrong, and speak up when they see others getting hurt. Doesn't that sound like a good friend?

Telling the truth is always the right thing to do. It's not always easy, but you're not alone! Ask God to help you speak truthfully, so you can be kind and loving—just the way He made you to be!

THOUGHT OF THE DAY

God is the truth expert—He always tells us the truth!

PRAY TODAY

Dear God, help me remember that telling the truth is the kind choice. I'm so glad everything You say is true! Amen.

PEACE FOR FREE

"Peace I leave with you; my peace I give you. I do not give to you as the world gives."

JOHN 14:27A NIV

If you want something from a store, you need to pay for it. But if you want peace from God, all you have to do is ask! It's ready any time you want it, and it doesn't cost a penny.

If you want to know what God's peace looks like, just get to know Him better! Pray and read your Bible every day. Memorize Bible verses, and share Bible stories with people you know. When you're close to God, you'll start to notice all the ways He blesses you and answers your prayers. He loves to give you peace!

THOUGHT OF THE DAY

When you spend time with God, His peace comes along too!

PRAY TODAY

Dear God, thanks for giving me Your peace for free! I am so glad You share good gifts with me. Amen.

GOD HEARS YOU

But God did listen! He paid attention to my prayer. Praise God, who did not ignore my prayer or withdraw his unfailing love from me.

PSALM 66:19–20 NLT

God promises He will always listen to your prayers. And He'll always answer you. But His answers may not always be what you expect.

Try this experiment at home: Make a list of things you want to pray about. Maybe it's feeling comfortable in a new school. Maybe you need help learning a skill, following the rules, or speaking up when something's wrong. Maybe you just want to feel closer to God! Pray every day, and once every week, check in with the list. You may be surprised by how God chose to answer your prayers!

THOUGHT OF THE DAY

The things you care about matter to God!

PRAY TODAY

Dear God, thank You for always hearing my prayers. I know You will answer when I talk to You! Amen.

DAY 233

HEAVEN IS WONDERFUL

"No eye has seen, no ear has heard, and no mind has imagined what God has prepared for those who love him."

1 CORINTHIANS 2:9B NLT

Do you wonder what heaven is like? The Bible uses picture language to tell us about it, saying the streets are gold, the light is like jewels, and there is beautiful music that sounds like rushing water. It also says there will be no sadness or sickness in heaven.

But those are just hints. Scripture tells us that heaven is more wonderful than we can even imagine! Because God loves us, He has prepared an amazing home where we will live with Him forever. You can be sure of one thing about heaven—it will be even better than you think!!

THOUGHT OF THE DAY

Heaven is real . . . and it's even more amazing than you can imagine!

PRAY TODAY

Dear God, thank You for making heaven where I can live with You forever. Amen.

HONOR YOUR PARENTS

"Honor your father and mother. Then you will live a long, full life in the land the LORD your God is giving you."

EXODUS 20:12 NLT

The Ten Commandments are God's rules for living a good life. They are all important, but did you know that there is only one with a promise? It's the fifth commandment. Read the verse above and see if you can find the promise.

Honoring your parents can mean doing what they ask without whining or talking back. It can also mean following their rules, helping them, and showing them you are grateful for all they do. God gives you parents so you can know how it feels to be loved. Loving them back is a way you can obey God and live a full, happy life together.

THOUGHT OF THE DAY

What are some ways you honor your parents?

PRAY TODAY

Dear God, thank You for my parents. Please help me to honor them, so they know how much I love them, and we can all be happy together. Amen.

HEARING EARS

"He who has ears to hear, let him hear."

MATTHEW 11:15 ESV

Do you know that you can hear something without really listening to it? Does you mom or dad ever say, "I just told you that!" Or maybe you heard a friend talking, but you don't remember what she said, because you weren't really listening.

Often, when Jesus told a story, He said: "He who has ears to hear, let him hear." What He meant was: Listen to what I'm saying and understand it. When you read the Bible, take time to hear and listen to what God is telling you. Pay attention. Then do what Jesus says.

THOUGHT OF THE DAY

Hear not only with your ears, but also with your mind.

PRAY TODAY

Dear God, I want to follow You. Please help me really listen to Your words. Amen.

GOD CAN DO ANYTHING

Jesus looked at them and said, "With man this is impossible, but with God all things are possible."

MATTHEW 19:26 NIV

Do you sometimes feel like you aren't good enough? Maybe you try and try to keep from saying unkind things, but sometimes you do anyway. Maybe you really want to tell the truth, but sometimes you don't.

God knows that even though we want to do what's right, we often fail. But Jesus tells us that when we can't do what we want, He is there to help us. He can do anything! Nothing is impossible for God. Next time you want to do the right thing, ask God to help you. With God, all things are possible!

THOUGHT OF THE DAY

When we are weak, Jesus is strong!

PRAY TODAY

Dear God, I'm so glad that You are always there. Please help me remember to ask You when I need help.

LOYAL FRIENDS

But Ruth said, "Do not urge me to leave you or to return from following you. For where you go I will go, and where you lodge I will lodge. Your people shall be my people, and your God my God."

RUTH 1:16 ESV

Good friends are so important. You enjoy playing, talking, and spending time together! But another quality that makes someone a good friend is loyalty. Loyalty means you are honest and trustworthy, and you stand up for your friend in good times and bad times.

It's easy to stay friends with someone who is happy all the time. But what do you do when a friend is sad or going through some hard times? If you are loyal, you always look for ways to encourage and support your friend. Loyal friends are there for each other!

THOUGHT OF THE DAY

Who has been a loyal friend to you? How are you loyal to your friends?

PRAY TODAY

Dear God, thank You for loyal friends. Please help me to be a true and loyal friend too. Amen.

HOW TO TREAT OTHERS

"Treat others just as you want to be treated."

LUKE 6:31 CEV

When someone has a toy you want, do you grab it? If someone gives you a gift, do you take it and never say thank you? At the dinner table, do you yell, "Hey, where's my food?" Even Mr. Nezzer knows that's not how to act!

Saying please and thank you shows respect for others. Asking politely and being grateful for what we have is just good manners. The Bible says to treat others the way we want to be treated. When we do, we are following Jesus' example.

THOUGHT OF THE DAY

Think about how you like to be treated, then treat others the same way!

PRAY TODAY

Dear God, please help me to remember to be thoughtful and kind. Amen.

POWER IN PRAISE

I will bless the LORD at all times; His praise shall continually be in my mouth.

PSALM 34:1 AMP

Some people wonder why they should praise God. They think, "God already knows how great He is, so why should I tell Him?" But here's the most important thing about praise: Praise reminds us how great God is! When we talk about the amazing things God does or sing about His goodness, we remember that He is more powerful than any fears or doubts we might feel.

God knows we often feel small or afraid. That's why He wants us to praise Him! As we speak of His greatness, power, and love, our bad feelings disappear!

THOUGHT OF THE DAY

Praising God builds our faith.

PRAY TODAY

Dear God, You are so great! Nothing can ever take Your love from me. Thank You. Amen.

DAY 240

A CHILD OF THE KING

And if children, then heirs—heirs of God and fellow heirs with Christ.

ROMANS 8:17A ESV

An heir is a child who has a right to what his or her parents own. The Bible says you are an heir of God. That means you are a part of God's family, and you can have all the wonderful things God has prepared for His children!

When you love Jesus and trust in Him, God gives you amazing gifts! He gives you love, peace, and joy. He gives you power and strength to overcome problems. When you belong to God's family, you are a princess because you are a child of the King!

THOUGHT OF THE DAY

You are precious to God, because you are His child!

PRAY TODAY

Dear God, I am so glad You chose me to be Your child. Thank You for loving me so much. Amen.

PICK ONE THING

What joy for those whose strength comes from the LORD.

PSALM 84:5A NLT

Have you ever woken up grumpy? On days like that, it's easy to stay in a bad mood all day. But that's no fun for anyone.

God wants you to feel His joy, even on grumpy days. So try starting small. Pick one thing that makes you happy. Did you eat something yummy for breakfast? Was your favorite shirt clean this morning? Did your pet do something silly? Once you pick something to be happy about, enjoy it! You might even find a few more things to be happy about along the way. God's joy is always ready for you!

THOUGHT OF THE DAY

Ask God to surprise you with joy each day!

PRAY TODAY

Dear God, some days I don't even feel like smiling. Please help me search for Your joy all the time. Amen.

DAY 242

YOU ARE POWERFUL

For the Kingdom of God is not just a lot of talk; it is living by God's power.

1 CORINTHIANS 4:20 NLT

Have you ever wanted a superpower? God gives each of His children an amazing power that they can use every day: to bring His kingdom to earth!

You do that by choosing actions that make God happy. Share the things you have. Invite someone new to play. Stand up for yourself and others. Take care of the earth. Tell the truth, even when it's tempting to lie. These things aren't always easy, so ask God to share His power with you. With His help, you can transform your home, your school, and your neighborhood into the kingdom of God!

THOUGHT OF THE DAY

Small actions add up to superpower!

PRAY TODAY

Dear God, You are super awesome! Please help me make kind, wise choices, so I can make the world look more like heaven. Amen.

THE GREATEST TEACHER

"I have given you an example to follow. Do as I have done to you."

JOHN 13:15 NLT

Do you have a teacher you love? Great teachers care about their students, help them discover new ideas, and encourage them when they make mistakes or try new things. And do you know the best teacher of all? Jesus!

Jesus loves to help His children grow. He told stories that made people think in new ways. He showed us how to love others and make good choices (even when it's hard). He promises to love you no matter what, and to help you try again when you mess up. With Jesus, there is always more to learn and more to love!

THOUGHT OF THE DAY

When you don't know what to do, check with Jesus—He'll help you!

PRAY TODAY

Dear Jesus, thank You for being the best teacher ever! Amen.

DAY 244

GOD ALWAYS LISTENS

Rejoice always! Pray constantly. Give thanks in everything, for this is God's will for you in Christ Jesus.

1 THESSALONIANS 5:16–18 HCSB

Sometimes we think about prayer as asking God for things. But prayer is much more than just asking. If you have a good friend, don't you love to tell them about all the fun and exciting things that are going on? Jesus wants to hear about those things too!

You can talk to Jesus out loud or in your mind. Tell Him about what makes you happy. Talk to Him about the things you are thankful for. When you spend time sharing joyful and grateful moments with Jesus, you will find it easy to pray.

THOUGHT OF THE DAY

What are some things you want to tell Jesus today?

PRAY TODAY

Dear God, I'm so glad You are always there. Thank You for listening to me. Amen.

A SPECIAL GIFT

You must encourage one another each day.

HEBREWS 3:13A CEV

There's a special gift you can give that doesn't cost anything. You don't have to wrap it up. And it doesn't even take up any space in your pocket. Do you know what it is? Encouragement!

Encouragement can be as simple as saying "hi" to someone who is feeling lonely. Or listening to a friend who is feeling sad. You can encourage someone with a hug or a smile. You can ask him to play with you or help her learn something new. Everyone needs encouragement. And here's a secret surprise: When you encourage someone else, the gift often comes back to you!

THOUGHT OF THE DAY

How will you encourage someone today?

PRAY TODAY

Dear God, please show me how to encourage others each day. Then help me to do it! Amen.

BE COURAGEOUS

"Be strong! Be courageous! Do not be afraid of them! For the Lord your God will be with you. He will neither fail you nor forsake you."

DEUTERONOMY 31:6 TLB

When you hear the word "courage" what do you think about? Superheroes who fight evil villains? Explorers who face wild animals?

Those aren't the only ways to be courageous. Courage is standing up for someone who is being teased. It is facing your fears of speaking up in class or trying something new. It's trying again when you make mistakes.

Here's some good news: the Bible says that when you need courage, you can always count on God to be with you. So be courageous!

THOUGHT OF THE DAY

When was a time you needed to be courageous?

PRAY TODAY

Dear God, I'm so glad that when I feel nervous or afraid I can always count on You to give me courage! Amen.

DAY 247

P.R.A.Y.

"Pray like this: Our Father in heaven, may your name be kept holy. May your Kingdom come soon. May your will be done on earth, as it is in heaven."

MATTHEW 6:9–10 NLT

Prayer is a way of talking to God. Sometimes we say prayers that we have memorized, and other times we just make up prayers. If you have trouble thinking about how to pray, here is a helpful trick. Just use the letters in the word PRAY!

P: Praise God for who He is and what He has done.

R: Repent. Ask God to forgive you for doing what you shouldn't or not doing what you should.

A: Ask God to help others.

Y: Ask God to help YOU.

Remember that you can always talk to God, and He will always hear you!

THOUGHT OF THE DAY

When do you enjoy praying?

PRAY TODAY

Dear God, thank You for always listening to me when I pray. Amen.

DAY 248

THE SECRET TO JOY

"You will live in joy and peace."

ISAIAH 55:12A NLT

Joy is a little word, but it makes a big difference in your life. And here's a secret for finding joy. Use the letters in the word to remember what brings real joy: J is for putting Jesus first. O is for showing His love to others. Y is for loving yourself too! J+O+Y=JOY.

If you remember this little formula, your life will be filled with joy and peace. When you love Jesus and share His love with others, you will discover that your heart fills up with good things. That's how to live the way God wants you to!

THOUGHT OF THE DAY

Living as God wants you to—it's Jesus, then others, then you!

PRAY TODAY

Dear God, please help me find real joy by putting You first. Amen.

SAYING WHAT'S TRUE

"These are the things you are to do: Speak the truth to each other."

ZECHARIAH 8:16 NIV

Speaking the truth means saying what really happened. If you take something and break it, when someone asks, "What happened?" you say, "I took it and I broke it." If you run into someone on the playground, you say, "I'm sorry I bumped into you. Are you OK?"

It's sometimes hard to tell the truth if you're afraid you might get into trouble or someone will be disappointed. But when you tell the truth, people know they can trust you. Good friends say what is true—even when it's hard to do.

THOUGHT OF THE DAY

Can you talk about a time when you told the truth?

PRAY TODAY

Dear God, I want to be someone who tells the truth. Please help me, even when it's hard to do. Amen.

A SPECIAL SIGN

"The rainbow that I have put in the sky will be my sign to you and to every living creature on earth."

GENESIS 9:12 CEV

Did you know that there is a special sign in the Bible that you can still see today? When the sun shines through raindrops, you can see a colorful arc of light in the sky. It is called a rainbow. God made the first rainbow as a sign of His loving promise to Noah's family. That first rainbow appeared thousands of years ago. And we can still see rainbows today. Whenever you see a rainbow, remember how much God loved Noah and how much He loves you too!

THOUGHT OF THE DAY

Draw a rainbow and put it in your room to remind you of God's love.

PRAY TODAY

Dear God, thank You for giving me beautiful rainbows to remind me of Your love. Amen.

DAY 251

A WONDERFUL BODY

I will praise You because I have been remarkably and wonderfully made. Your works are wonderful, and I know this very well.

PSALM 139:14 HCSB

Did you know that every minute your heart beats about 100 times and you breathe in and out about 25 times? The most amazing thing is that you never even have to think about it! You don't have to remind your heart to beat. You don't have to remember to breathe.

Didn't God make you a wonderful body? Your heart, lungs, and many other parts keep working on their own so you can focus on things like learning or making friends! So be sure to make healthy choices for your body. It's one way of saying "thank You" to God for this great gift!

THOUGHT OF THE DAY

What are some things you do to take care of your body?

PRAY TODAY

Dear God, thank You for giving me such a wonderful body. Help me to take good care of it every day. Amen.

CHOOSE TO PRAY

Do not worry about anything, but pray and ask God for everything you need, always giving thanks.

PHILIPPIANS 4:6 NCV

When a thought pops into your head, you have a choice. You can worry about it or you can choose to pray about it. Did you meet a new friend, but you wonder if they want to play with you? Ask God to help you be friendly. At night, do you sometimes feel a little afraid when the light is off? Ask God to help you feel safe and cozy in your bed. Any time you talk to God, you are praying. He loves to hear and answer your prayers. Choosing to pray helps our worries go away!

THOUGHT OF THE DAY

What is something you can pray about today?

PRAY TODAY

Dear God, thanks for always hearing my prayers and helping me not to worry. Amen.

RIGHT ON TIME

He has made everything beautiful in its time.

ECCLESIASTES 3:11 NIV

Sometimes it feels like God moves really slowly. Sometimes it might even seem like He's not doing anything! But don't worry. God is always at work, helping you grow and learn. He has wonderful plans for you!

Talk to God about the things you want. Tell Him how hard it is to wait and ask for His help! Then watch for Him during your day. Did a friend say something encouraging? Are you getting closer to mastering a new skill? Was today happier than yesterday? God won't let you down. When you trust Him, He'll show up right on time!

THOUGHT OF THE DAY

God will give you exactly what you need at exactly the right time.

PRAY TODAY

Dear God, sometimes it's hard to see You working. Help me trust that Your timing is the best timing. Amen.

DAY 254

HEAR YOUR FAITH

So faith comes from hearing, that is, hearing the Good News about Christ.

ROMANS 10:17 NLT

Faith means believing in something we can't see. It's not always easy. But the Bible gives us a simple way to have more faith: hear the Good News of Jesus!

When you hear about all the things Jesus said and did, you'll start to understand His love for you. You can hear about Jesus at church, of course. But you don't have to wait for Sunday! Ask your mom or dad to help you read Bible stories every day. Listen to worship songs, or make up your own! Every time you hear about Jesus your faith will grow a little more.

THOUGHT OF THE DAY

A devotional book like this one is a great way to hear the Good News too!

PRAY TODAY

Dear God, when I hear about Jesus, please help me really listen. I want my faith to grow! Amen.

CAREFUL LISTENING

Listen carefully to wisdom; set your mind on understanding.

PROVERBS 2:2 NCV

Every day you hear many different things. Some things are true, and some are not. If you are a careful listener, you will be able to understand who is telling you the truth and who is not. God wants us to listen to people who can be trusted.

Some trustworthy people are your parents, or your grandparents. Others are good teachers who help you learn and good coaches who help you play better. Good friends help you grow and understand new things too. When you listen to wise, kind people, you will discover true things that will help you become who God wants you to be.

THOUGHT OF THE DAY

Who is someone you know who can be trusted to tell the truth?

PRAY TODAY

Dear God, help me remember to be a careful listener and to grow to understand the truth. Amen.

BE A LIGHT

"You are the light of the world. A town built on a hill cannot be hidden. . . . Let your light shine before others, that they may see your good deeds and glorify your Father in heaven."

MATTHEW 5:14–16 NIV

If you are hiking in the dark, you cannot see where to go. But if you have a flashlight, you can turn it on. Then you can see the right way to go! In the Bible, Jesus calls His followers "the light of the world." What that means is that when we do what Jesus says, we become like a light, shining in the dark, so others can see the way to go.

When you live Jesus' way, you help others see God. You become a "light" where you live, play, and learn, by doing the right thing.

THOUGHT OF THE DAY

How could you be a "light" for someone you know?

PRAY TODAY

Dear God, please help me to shine brightly for You so others know You love them too. Amen.

DANIEL'S CHOICE

But Daniel made up his mind that he would not defile himself . . .

DANIEL 1:8 NASB

Daniel was a Bible hero who had to make some hard choices. He had to decide whether he would obey God's laws or obey the laws of a bad king named Darius. If Daniel chose to obey God, King Darius would get mad! It was a scary choice, but Daniel decided to obey God instead of the king.

Angry King Darius threw Daniel into a pit with hungry lions. But God shut the lions' mouths and protected Daniel! Then Darius knew that Daniel's God was more powerful than any king on earth! God took care of Daniel because Daniel chose to obey Him.

THOUGHT OF THE DAY

Choosing to obey God isn't always easy, but it is always the right thing to do.

PRAY TODAY

Dear God, help me make good choices each day. I want to follow Jesus and do what is right. Amen.

DAY 258

RIGHT BESIDE YOU

"Fear not, for I am with you; Be not dismayed, for I am your God. I will strengthen you."

ISAIAH 41:10A NKJV

When you're with your friends or family, how do you feel? It's easy to feel happy, confident, and even brave with people who love you. The good news is, you can feel that way all the time! That's because God is always with you.

There may be times you feel lonely, but God is right beside you. And He says you never have to feel afraid or worried, because He'll never leave! So ask for His help. Tell Him your thoughts and feelings. Then trust Him to make you strong!

THOUGHT OF THE DAY

God will never try to hide. He's forever by your side!

PRAY TODAY

Dear God, I love You! Thank You for being with me all day, every day. Amen.

DAY 259

SLOW YOUR ANGER

Don't let your spirit rush to be angry, for anger abides in the heart of fools.

ECCLESIASTES 7:9 HCSB

There's nothing wrong with feeling angry sometimes. But if you get mad really easily, that's no fun for anyone. Good news: God can help slow down your anger!

For example, imagine you want to play soccer today, but your friend doesn't. That might make you feel angry! But instead of yelling or stomping away, take a breath. What are some ways you both could have fun? Is there something else you love to do together? It takes practice, but God can help you turn a quick temper into quick problem-solving!

THOUGHT OF THE DAY

Don't rush into feeling mad. Find a way you'll all be glad!

PRAY TODAY

Dear God, sometimes I get angry so quickly, I can't stop my words. Please help me slow down. I can do anything with Your help! Amen.

GOD'S PERFECT TIMING

"Who knows? Maybe you were made queen for just such a time as this."

ESTHER 4:14 MSG

Queen Esther was very brave. She trusted God and always tried to listen to Him. One day, Esther overheard a plan to hurt her family and the people she loved. She wanted to stop it, but she was afraid she would get hurt too. Her cousin, Mordecai, reminded her that God's plans are perfect. Maybe God had even made her queen for this very moment! Queen Esther spoke up to the king and stopped the evil plans.

God has given you your friends, your family, and your neighborhood for a reason. Look around. Who can you help today?

THOUGHT OF THE DAY

God's plans always happen at the right time—God's time!

PRAY TODAY

Dear God, please help me trust You always. Your plans and timing are perfect! Amen.

ASK FOR PEACE

"Peace I leave with you; my peace I give you. I do not give to you as the world gives. Do not let your hearts be troubled and do not be afraid."

JOHN 14:27 NIV

Jesus knows that sometimes we worry or feel afraid. He understands when we are shy or upset. But Jesus also knows how to help when we feel like this: He gives us His peace!

Jesus can make our hearts feel calm when we are worried. His peace helps us feel less afraid. He is always with us and promises to give us peace when we ask Him for it. When you are upset, ask Jesus to fill your heart with His peace and calm. Then trust Him to do it.

THOUGHT OF THE DAY

Can you think of a time when you needed Jesus to fill your heart with peace?

PRAY TODAY

Dear Jesus, thank You for the peace You give me. Help me to remember to ask You for it whenever I worry or feel afraid. Amen.

USE YOUR GIFTS

God has given each of you a gift from his great variety of spiritual gifts. Use them well to serve one another.

1 PETER 4:10 NLT

You are a wonderful, special creation! God made you different from anyone else on Earth. He gave you your smile, your laugh, your likes, and even your dislikes. And He also gave you spiritual gifts!

Spiritual gifts are special abilities God gave you to use for Him. Maybe you are a terrific listener, and others feel comforted when they talk with you. Maybe you like to read Scripture in church. Do you like to share Jesus' story with your friends? Or sing in a choir? Ask God to show you what gifts He's given you. Then use them to praise God—and help others!

THOUGHT OF THE DAY

There is only one you! How do you love to praise God and serve people?

PRAY TODAY

Dear God, please show me the ways You've made me special. I want to use my gifts well! Amen.

GOOD INGREDIENTS

"A good man brings good things out of the good stored up in him."

MATTHEW 12:35A NIV

Have you ever had chocolate chip cookies? Imagine if you put pickles in the batter instead of chocolate chips! Yuck! But when you use the right ingredients, you can't help but make a delicious treat.

It's the same with good deeds. Good deeds are kind actions that are like treats for the heart. And in order to make delicious heart-treats, you need to start with the best ingredient: goodness! Think kindly of others and never spread gossip. Search for good things in everything that happens. Thank God all the time! When goodness fills your heart, you can make a whole batch of good deeds!

THOUGHT OF THE DAY

Stock up on goodness today, so you can serve up good deeds tomorrow!

PRAY TODAY

Dear God, please help me fill my heart with good ingredients, so I can bless others! Amen.

DAY 264

LET'S PARTY!

A cheerful heart has a continual feast.

PROVERBS 15:15B HCSB

Isn't it hard to go home when you're having fun at a party? Well, God says that having a cheerful heart is just like a great party—except you never have to leave!

You can have a cheerful heart by noticing all the gifts God has given you. Not just the things you ask for—like presents on Christmas or pizza day at school. Look at what He gives you every day! There's warm sunshine, bright rainbows, funny friends, a loving family, sparkly stars, and yummy food. When you're praising God, your joy will never end. And neither will the party in your heart!

THOUGHT OF THE DAY

With God, party time is all the time!

PRAY TODAY

Dear God, please give me a cheerful heart so I can always party with You! Amen.

GOD'S LOVE IS FOREVER

But for those who honor the LORD, his love lasts forever, and his goodness endures for all generations.

PSALM 103:17 GNT

Every spring and summer, flowers bloom with bright colors and trees fill with green leaves. Every fall, leaves turn red and orange and brown. Then, winter snow might even cover the ground until spring warms it up again! The world is always changing. And so are you! You are learning new things, making new friends, and even growing out of old clothes! But one thing never changes. God's love is the same today as it was yesterday. It will be the same tomorrow and next week and next year. It will never fade away and you cannot lose it. It's yours forever!

THOUGHT OF THE DAY

The love of God is always there. You'll never lose His tender care.

PRAY TODAY

Dear God, thank You for loving me now and forever. I am so glad I'm Your child. Amen.

THE KEY TO HAPPINESS

Rejoice always! Pray constantly. Give thanks in everything, for this is God's will for you in Christ Jesus.

1 THESSALONIANS 5:16–18 HCSB

God gives us three secrets to a happy life. First, praise God for what He's done. These can be small things, like the way He's made flowers smell so sweet, or big things, like giving you a loving family. Second, pray all the time. That doesn't mean you should walk around with your eyes closed and hands folded! Just talk to God during your day. And third, give thanks no matter what. Even if things don't go your way, look for something to be thankful for anyway. When you follow God's three steps, you'll be surprised how much happiness you'll find!

THOUGHT OF THE DAY

Find a reason to praise God and a reason to thank Him. Then pray and tell Him what you found!

PRAY TODAY

Dear God, there is so much to be glad about! Help me remember to pray, praise, and say thanks every day. Amen.

WORSHIP ALL THE TIME

Oh come, let us worship and bow down; let us kneel before the LORD, our Maker!

PSALM 95:6 ESV

Some people think they have to be in a church to worship God. But did you know that you can worship God wherever you are? Worshipping means using whatever you have, wherever you are, to honor and please God. You can worship God at the park by treating others the way God wants you to. You can worship God at home by being a helper and respecting your parents. You can worship God anywhere when you pray and sing and give thanks for all the amazing things He has done! Take time to worship God every day.

THOUGHT OF THE DAY

Can you name two ways you will worship God today?

PRAY TODAY

Dear God, You are so wonderful. I love You and I want to please You today in all I do! Amen.

PLAY YOUR PART

And above all these put on love, which binds everything together in perfect harmony.

COLOSSIANS 3:14 ESV

When everyone in an orchestra plays their part on their instrument, the orchestra sounds beautiful. They are playing in harmony. When everyone on a team or in a family or in a classroom does their part, they are working in harmony. The team plays well. The family gets along. The classmates learn more. It's important to work and play in harmony with others. But that takes love. We need to learn to love each other and then celebrate our differences. No one can do every part, but when we each do our own part, everyone succeeds!

THOUGHT OF THE DAY

What part do you play in your family or classroom?

PRAY TODAY

Thank You, Lord, for making each person special. Please help me to do my part well so we can work together in harmony! Amen.

TRUE LOVE

My children, our love should not be only words and talk. Our love must be true love. And we should show that love by what we do.

1 JOHN 3:18 ICB

Love is more than just words. After all, if you say you love someone, then refuse to help or never share what you have, do you think they will believe your words are true? No! You have to show your love as well as speak it. God shows His love for us through good gifts like His beautiful world and His peace and joy. You can show love for your family by helping without being asked. You can love your friends by encouraging them and cheering when they do well. Find ways to show true love each day with words and actions.

THOUGHT OF THE DAY

What are some ways you can show true love today?

PRAY TODAY

Thank You, God, for loving me. Please help me show my love to others by what I do each day. Amen.

DON'T WAIT

"All of us must quickly carry out the tasks assigned us by the one who sent me, for there is little time left before the night falls and all work comes to an end."

JOHN 9:4 TLB

Laura promised to help Junior Asparagus learn to ride his scooter before his birthday. But she kept putting it off. One day she was busy playing ball. Another day she got interested in reading a book. When Junior reminded her of her promise, she said, "I'll do it later." Then it was Junior's birthday. He felt sad because he had wanted to ride his scooter all the way to the park for his party. Laura was sorry she had disappointed her friend. She decided that next time she made a promise to help someone she wouldn't wait. She would do it right away!

THOUGHT OF THE DAY

How can you help someone right now instead of waiting?

PRAY TODAY

Dear Jesus, thank You for always helping me. Please help me not to wait when I could be helping others. Amen.

TODAY'S A GREAT DAY!

This is the day that the LORD has made. Let us rejoice and be glad today!

PSALM 118:24 NCV

When you think of celebrations, what do you think of? Birthdays and holidays? Maybe a big accomplishment, like winning a baseball game? Well, guess what? The Bible says every single day is a reason to celebrate, simply because God made it! Every day, God makes the sun rise and the birds sing. He makes the rain fall so plants can grow. He turns caterpillars into butterflies and decorates the night sky with stars. Even when things don't go your way, God is with you, all day every day. So celebrate! Because God made this a great day.

THOUGHT OF THE DAY

Can you name three things that make today great? Praise God for them!

PRAY TODAY

Dear God, thank You for today! You have made a beautiful world for me. Amen.

DAY 272

SPEAK FROM YOUR HEART

"The mouth speaks the things that are in the heart."

MATTHEW 12:34B ICB

Have you ever said something you wish you could take back? Unkind words make others sad. And they don't make you feel great, either! But God has some advice to help you. Fill your heart with good things!

The Bible says that whatever is in your heart will come out in the things you say. So if you spend all your time feeling angry or selfish, your words will probably be hurtful. But if you look for ways to be thankful, helpful, and kind, your words will show all those things too! So today, try turning your thoughts from mad to glad. Everyone will hear the difference!

THOUGHT OF THE DAY

It's so much easier to be kind when only good things fill your mind!

PRAY TODAY

Dear God, please help me fill my heart with good things. I want my words to make people happy! Amen.

WISHING OR HOPING?

May the God of hope fill you with all joy and peace as you trust in him, so that you may overflow with hope by the power of the Holy Spirit.

ROMANS 15:13 NIV

Have you ever wished for something? Sometimes people make wishes on a birthday candle or on a star. They think that if they wish really, really hard they will get what they want. But after they finish wishing, they start worrying that their wishes won't come true!

Hoping is different from wishing. The Bible tells us that hope is putting our trust in God, who loves us and always wants the best for us. When we trust in God to give us His very best, we can stop worrying. Hope fills us with joy and peace instead!

THOUGHT OF THE DAY

Trusting in God will help you rest, because He gives you what is best!

PRAY TODAY

Dear God, I am so thankful I don't need to worry, because my hope is in You. Amen.

DAY 274

YOUR SPECIAL GIFT

This is why I remind you to keep using the gift God gave you . . .

2 TIMOTHY 1:6A NCV

Isn't it fun to open a gift? And it's even more fun to use it! Did you know that God gives each of us gifts? But they're not in boxes or bags. God's gifts are special abilities we can use to become the person He's created us to be.

Maybe you love to draw, or are good at music, reading, or math. Perhaps you're great at helping people or listening. There are all kinds of gifts God gives His children. Ask for His help to discover them and use them as you grow!

THOUGHT OF THE DAY

What do you think your gift from God might be? How can you use it as you grow?

PRAY TODAY

Dear God, thank You for giving me special gifts. Help me to work at using my gift for You and others. Amen.

SNEAKY GOODNESS

None of you should look out just for your own good. Each of you should also look out for the good of others.

PHILIPPIANS 2:4 NIRV

Some people get a lot of attention for doing good deeds. But God doesn't care about attention. He wants you to choose kind actions just because you want to help others.

Here's a fun way to do God's kind of goodness. Think of someone who needs to be cheered up. Then make something special for them—you could draw a pretty picture or maybe ask a parent to help you bake a yummy treat! Now leave the gift somewhere they'll find it, but don't tell anyone who it's from. They will feel happier and loved. But only you and God will know about your sneaky goodness!

THOUGHT OF THE DAY

How would you feel if someone gave you a sneaky gift?

PRAY TODAY

Dear God, please show me how to help others every day, even when no one's paying attention! Amen.

TWO EARS AND ONE MOUTH

My dear brothers and sisters, always be willing to listen and slow to speak.

JAMES 1:19 NCV

Someone once said that we have two ears and one mouth, because we should listen twice as much as we talk! That's a funny way to say it, but did you know that the Bible also says we should listen more than we talk? Why do you think that is?

Listening is how we learn and understand. And it's also a way to show we care about someone. If we speak without listening, we might hurt someone's feelings! Listening first is God's way to show respect and love for others. Give it a try!

THOUGHT OF THE DAY

Listen to hear what others say. Then when you speak, others will listen to you!

PRAY TODAY

Dear God, sometimes it is hard for me to listen. Please help me give others time to speak before I do. Amen.

GOD'S GOOD PLANS

"I know what I am planning for you," says the Lord. "I have good plans for you, not plans to hurt you. I will give you hope and a good future."

JEREMIAH 29:11 NCV

Do you like thinking about what you will be when you grow up? Maybe you even enjoy pretending to be a firefighter, a ballerina, a teacher, an astronaut, or something else. It's wonderful to dream about—and even plan for!—what you will be one day.

You may not know just what you will become, but you can be sure that God has great plans for you. He loves you and wants only what is best for you. Pray every day and ask God to show you what He wants you to be. You can always trust God's plans.

THOUGHT OF THE DAY

What do you think you will do? Trust in God's good plans for you!

PRAY TODAY

Dear God, I am so glad that You have good plans for me. Please help me to follow Your ways each day. Amen.

HOORAY FOR FRIENDS!

Every time I think of you, I give thanks to my God.

PHILIPPIANS 1:3 NLT

Friends are some of God's greatest gifts. A good friend can cheer you up when you feel sad, or help you finish a hard job. Friends can show you how to do something new. They can tell you funny stories and laugh at your jokes! And you can never have too many friends. There's always room for more!

It feels great to have good friends. So take time to thank God today for the ones He's given to you. And don't forget to be a good friend too!

THOUGHT OF THE DAY

Who is one of your good friends? How can you show you're thankful for their friendship?

PRAY TODAY

Dear God, thank You for my friends. Help me to be a good friend to each one! Amen.

STAY CONNECTED

"Yes, I am the Vine; you are the branches. Whoever lives in me and I in him shall produce a large crop of fruit. For apart from me you can't do a thing."

JOHN 15:5 TLB

Have you ever picked apples? You can fill your bucket or basket in just a few minutes when the branches are loaded with delicious fruit. But if a branch breaks off the tree it will never produce another apple. The branch must stay connected to the tree for apples to grow. The Bible says we are like those branches. We can do wonderful things when we stay connected to Jesus. You can do that by spending time reading your Bible, praying, and asking Jesus to help you every day. Then watch your "fruit" grow!

THOUGHT OF THE DAY

Name some ways you can connect with Jesus today.

PRAY TODAY

Dear Jesus, thank You for helping me to learn and grow. Please keep me close to You each day. Amen.

DO AND GROW

Be doers of the word, and not hearers only.

JAMES 1:22 NKJV

What if your teacher told you how to do a math problem, but you never did one yourself? What if your mom or dad showed how to ride a bike, but you never tried it? If you don't do something with all the things you learn, you won't grow! It's the same way when we hear God's words in the Bible. If we don't do what the words say, we won't grow as believers. God tells us to be kind, share, and help others. When we do these things, our faith grows stronger, and so does our friendship with God!

THOUGHT OF THE DAY

What is something God has told you to do?

PRAY TODAY

Dear God, thank You for telling me the right way to live. Please help me to do what You say. Amen.

GIVE GOOD THINGS

"Freely you have received; freely give."

MATTHEW 10:8B NIV

We each have been given so much. Not just presents on special occasions, but also kindness and love from friends and family. Why does God allow us to have good things we enjoy? The Bible says it's because God wants us to give good things to others! You can give some of your clothes, books, and toys to children who don't have much. You can give your time to help a neighbor. You can share your knowledge by helping a younger child learn something new. You have so much to give! How will you be a giver today?

THOUGHT OF THE DAY

Learning to give is the best way to live!

PRAY TODAY

Dear God, thank You for giving me so much! Please help me learn to be a joyful giver. Amen.

STOP SPREADING ANGER

A gentle answer turns away anger, but a sharp word causes anger.

PROVERBS 15:1 NLV

When someone is mad, they often use angry words. Then the other person gets angry and shouts back. Pretty soon, everyone is upset and nothing has been solved! God knows that we all feel angry sometimes, but He wants us to keep that anger from spreading. How do we do that? Today's verse gives us a clue—use gentle words! It is hard to do, but practicing makes it easier. Try using gentle words like "I'm sorry," "I need some time to think," or "I can't talk about this right now," and you can turn away anger before it spreads.

THOUGHT OF THE DAY

Why should we stop anger from spreading?

PRAY TODAY

Dear God, when I'm angry, please help me to use gentle words instead of angry ones. Thank You. Amen.

KEEP GOD'S COMMANDS

This is how we are sure that we have come to know Him: by keeping His commands.

1 JOHN 2:3 HCSB

Do you know what a command is? It is an order or direction that tells you what to do or what not to do. Commands like "don't walk" and "stop" help keep us safe. Commands like "come in" and "keep out" tell us where to go. In the Bible there are special commands that help us know who God is and how He wants us to live. God says to "tell the truth," "give to those in need," "love one another," and "forgive." When we keep God's commands, we grow in faith and get to know Him better.

THOUGHT OF THE DAY

What is one of God's commands you can keep today?

PRAY TODAY

Dear God, thank You for giving me Your commands. Please help me to keep them so I can know You better. Amen.

DAY 284

LOOK FOR GOD

"But from there you will search for the Lord your God, and you will find Him when you seek Him with all your heart and all your soul."

DEUTERONOMY 4:29 HCSB

God does not hide from you. He promises that if you look for Him, you will find Him. But how do you look for God? Ask Him to show Himself to you: in the Bible, in other people, and in nature. Then be on the lookout for what is true, what is loving, and what is beautiful. God's truth can be found in the Bible. God's love can be found in the kindness of family and friends. And God's beauty can be seen in the world all around you. When you look for God, you will find Him!

THOUGHT OF THE DAY

Where will you look for God today?

PRAY TODAY

Thank You, God, for promising to always be with me. Help me look for You every day. Amen.

DAY 285

NEVER SEPARATED

And I am convinced that nothing can ever separate us from God's love. . . . No power in the sky above or in the earth below—indeed, nothing in all creation will ever be able to separate us from the love of God that is revealed in Christ Jesus our Lord.

ROMANS 8:38–39 NLT

If you have ever moved or had a friend move away, you know the lonely feeling of being separated from someone special. Maybe you had a pet that got lost or died. That's a lonely feeling too. Jesus makes a wonderful promise to us. He says He will never let us be separated from Him. His love is stronger than anything on earth or in the heavens. No matter where we go, how we feel, or what we do, we cannot be separated from God's love for us! He is always with us!

THOUGHT OF THE DAY

God's love is stronger than anything!

PRAY TODAY

Thank You that nothing can separate me from Your love, God. I'm so glad You are always with me. Amen.

DAY 286

CHANGE YOUR MIND

"Those who are pure in their thinking are happy. They will be with God."

MATTHEW 5:8 ICB

The Bible says we can choose how we think. If it rains on your birthday, you can choose to be mad or think of a way to enjoy your day anyway. If your friend gets sick and can't play, you can choose to stay grumpy all day or think about a way to help your friend feel better. When someone breaks your toy, you can choose to say mean words or to forgive them. With God's help, you can change your mind. This week try using your mind to think good thoughts at tough times. I wonder if you'll feel happier!

THOUGHT OF THE DAY

When you choose to think about how to make things better, you're thinking like God!

PRAY TODAY

Dear God, I want to think like You. Please help me learn to change my mind. Amen.

PRAISE GOD

"Praise the name of God forever and ever, for he has all wisdom and power."

DANIEL 2:20 NLT

The Bible says it's important to praise God. That's because praising God reminds us that He can do anything and that He loves each and every person. We praise God when we tell Him we know how great He is. We also praise Him when we thank Him for being loving, wise, and powerful. You can sing songs to Him, pray, raise your hands in worship, or sit quietly and think about how wonderful He is. And you can praise Him anytime, anywhere! So why not spend some time in praise today?

THOUGHT OF THE DAY

What is something you can praise God about right now?

PRAY TODAY

Dear God, I'm glad You are so powerful, wise, and kind. Thank You for loving me. Amen.

YOU CAN BE SURE

For the LORD will be your confidence, And will keep your foot from being caught.

PROVERBS 3:26 NKJV

This verse talks about "confidence." That's a word that means being sure of something. If you learn to kick a ball, ride a scooter, or sing a song, you become confident you can do it well. But there are other things you might not feel so sure about—like how you will do at school, whether someone will be your friend, or what will happen tomorrow. Today's Bible verse reminds us that God will be our confidence in any situation. Any time you aren't sure about something, remember that you can be sure that God is always with you!

THOUGHT OF THE DAY

What's something you aren't sure about? How will you trust God for help?

PRAY TODAY

Dear God, thank You that You are always with me. Please help me put my confidence in You. Amen.

REAL HAPPINESS

Be happy with what you have. God has said, "I will never leave you or let you be alone."

HEBREWS 13:5B NLV

What makes you happy? Maybe your friends, family, or pets? Or winning your favorite game, eating a special treat, or just playing with your favorite toys? Every good thing you have is a gift from God, and of course those things make you feel happy! But there's a special happiness that doesn't depend on what you have or who you know. God says He will never leave you or let you be alone. He knows you, loves you, and will always guide you. Things and people can make you feel happy for a while, but knowing God loves you can make you happy forever! That's real happiness!

THOUGHT OF THE DAY

How does knowing God loves you make you happy?

PRAY TODAY

Dear God, I'm so happy that You are always with me! Thank You for loving me so much. Amen.

PRAISE GOD ALWAYS!

My mouth is filled with your praise, and with your glory all the day.

PSALM 71:8 ESV

When you really love something, it's hard to stop talking about it. That's how we should feel about God!

Think about all the wonderful promises God has made. He will never leave you. He has big plans for you. He made you with special care, and gave you amazing gifts and talents. What an awesome God! So let's praise Him! Sing songs about His love, and share His greatness with your friends. Say prayers of thanks. You can even make up dances for Him! When you praise God, you remind your heart how great He is. So praise Him all day, every day!

THOUGHT OF THE DAY

Praise makes God happy—and it will make you happy too!

PRAY TODAY

Dear God, I love You! You give me all I need and You care for me so much. Thank You! Amen.

THE BEST TEACHER

"Teacher, I will follow you wherever you go."

MATTHEW 8:19 ESV

Do you have a favorite teacher at school or church? What makes them a good teacher? Great teachers patiently help solve problems and explain things in fun or creative ways! And the best teachers also live as good examples.

The Bible tells us that Jesus was the very best teacher ever. He not only taught people how to live, but He loved them. He listened carefully to their problems. He treated each person with respect. And Jesus always lived so people could follow His perfect example. When you learn to do what Jesus teaches, you are following the very best teacher!

THOUGHT OF THE DAY

What are some lessons you have learned from the way Jesus lived?

PRAY TODAY

Dear Jesus, thank You for being my best teacher. I am so glad that You love me and help me with every problem. Amen.

DAY 292

SERVE WITH A SMILE

Never be lazy, but work hard and serve the Lord enthusiastically.

ROMANS 12:11 NLT

God wants you to serve cheerfully and to be excited about the work you do! But how can you do that when you'd rather be doing anything else? Make it fun! Turn on some music and transform clean-up time into a dance party! Maybe you can sing a silly song to cheer up your brother. You could even pretend you DO feel like working! Tell yourself "I just love setting the table! Forks are my favorite!" Get into a silly mood, and you'll serve with a smile every time!

THOUGHT OF THE DAY

Do you have chores? How can you make them fun?

PRAY TODAY

Dear God, I know You like it best when I serve with a smile. Please help me be happy to help others! Amen.

A HAPPY HOME

"Honor your father and mother. Then you will live a long, full life in the land the LORD your God is giving you."

EXODUS 20:12 NLT

God gave us a list of good rules called the Ten Commandments. But only one of these rules comes with a promise. It's in today's verse! God says that life will be best when you are kind and respectful to your parents.

How does that work? It's simple! If you show respect to people, you'll get respect too. When you treat people with kindness, everyone is happier. When you get angry, choosing to speak calmly and listen well will help you make peace more easily. And when all this happens in a family, what a happy home you'll have!

THOUGHT OF THE DAY

Your family's a gift, so treat them with care. Be kind and respectful, and peace will be there!

PRAY TODAY

Dear God, thank You for my family. Please help me honor them every day. Amen.

FILLED WITH GOD

So we will not be afraid even if the earth shakes, or the mountains fall into the sea.

PSALM 46:2 NCV

It's normal to feel afraid sometimes. But the Bible says God is our protector. He is a safe place, and His love is forever. So when God fills your heart, there's no room for fear to live!

You can fill your heart with God by praying each day and learning Bible stories. God has been helping people feel brave since way back in Bible times! It might help to choose a song to sing each time you feel scared, like "Jesus Loves Me." When God's in your heart, scary feelings might creep in, but they can't stick around!

THOUGHT OF THE DAY

The words "fear not" appear 365 times in the Bible—that's once for every day of the year!

PRAY TODAY

Dear God, please fill my heart so fear has no place to stay. Amen!

CARING THROUGH SHARING

Give generously, for your gifts will return to you later.

ECCLESIASTES 11:1 TLB

Being generous means sharing what you have with others, even when it's hard. Sometimes that looks like giving away the money in your piggy bank to help feed people who can't buy food. Other times, it's donating old toys and books to your church or even splitting your snack in half to share with a friend who forgot hers. You might not always feel like being generous, but once you try it, it feels pretty great. In fact, it can be fun! See if you can find new ways to be generous each day. God promises to bless you for caring through sharing.

THOUGHT OF THE DAY

Can you think of a time when someone was generous to you?

PRAY TODAY

Dear God, it's fun to make others happy! Help me to be generous with all the blessings You've given me. Amen.

JOY FROM GOD

But let all those rejoice who put their trust in You; Let them ever shout for joy, because You defend them; Let those also who love Your name Be joyful in You.

PSALM 5:11 NKJV

You might think being a king would be super fun. But King David's life wasn't always easy. In the book of Psalms, he wrote about feeling sad, confused, and even angry. But since he never stopped trusting God, he was still able to rejoice!

You can be joyful like King David too. That doesn't mean you need to be happy all the time. Sometimes it's hard to feel happy, isn't it? Joy comes from God and it's bigger than happiness. It means you trust that God will work things out, and you're excited for His plans. God can give you joy today. Just ask!

THOUGHT OF THE DAY

Give God your trust, and He'll give you His joy!

PRAY TODAY

Dear God, I want to have Your joy in my heart! Help me trust You more and more each day. Amen.

TRY AGAIN

The LORD says, "Forget what happened before, and do not think about the past. Look at the new thing I am going to do. It is already happening. Don't you see it?"

ISAIAH 43:18–19A NCV

When was the last time you tried something new? Did you do it perfectly the first time? Of course not! Doing something well takes practice! When you try new things, you'll probably make a lot of mistakes. You might feel discouraged. You might even want to stop. But God says you should keep going!

What can you do differently next time? What can you learn from last time? God is with you, and He will use your mistakes to help you get better. But only if you keep working. So get back out there and try again!

THOUGHT OF THE DAY

With God's help, every mistake can become a wonderful lesson!

PRAY TODAY

Dear God, sometimes I get frustrated when I can't do something right. Please help me try again instead of giving up! Amen.

GOD CAN DO IT

Jesus looked at them intently, then said, "Without God, it is utterly impossible. But with God everything is possible."

MARK 10:27 TLB

The Bible tells us that when God's people were wandering in a desert without food and water, they called out to God. He made a special kind of food called manna fall from the sky. He even made water flow out of a rock. God can do what we think is impossible!

God wants to help you too. When you have a problem that is really hard or when you are afraid, things may seem impossible. But God can help. He loves you and wants to do wonderful things for you. Talk to God, then watch to see what He can do!

THOUGHT OF THE DAY

What is your favorite Bible story about God doing impossible things?

PRAY TODAY

Dear God, I am so glad that nothing is impossible for You! Thank You for loving me and helping me. Amen.

TURN ON THE LIGHT

Then Jesus spoke to them again, saying, "I am the light of the world. He who follows Me shall not walk in darkness, but have the light of life."

JOHN 8:12 NKJV

Imagine being stuck in a dark room. Would you feel confused? Scared? Now imagine you have a flashlight. You can see everything! The darkness cannot hide from you and your flashlight.

Bad feelings are like being in a dark room. When you're worried, angry, or jealous, it's hard to notice anything else. But when you think of Jesus' promises, it's like having a powerful flashlight. Remember His all-the-time love. Thank Him for the good gifts He's given you. Look for ways to show love to others. Dark feelings are no match for Jesus' light!

THOUGHT OF THE DAY

Nothing lights up your heart like remembering Jesus' love!

PRAY TODAY

Dear Jesus, I'm so glad You shine Your light everywhere. Help me remember Your love all the time! Amen.

LET YOUR PATIENCE SHOW

Let your patience show itself perfectly in what you do. Then you will be perfect and complete and will have everything you need.

JAMES 1:4 NCV

Patience means waiting without getting angry. Sometimes that means waiting for something you want, like a birthday party or someone to play a game with you. And sometimes it means taking the time to do something well.

When you are learning something new, be patient with yourself! Try not to get discouraged if your drawings don't look like you'd hoped or if you can't play a sport as well as someone else. Keep trying! Let your patience show, and you'll get a little better each day.

THOUGHT OF THE DAY

Sometimes it helps to take a quick break, and then try again later!

PRAY TODAY

Dear God, sometimes I get so frustrated. Please help me be patient with myself so I can get better at new things. Amen.

DAY 301

BIG PROMISES

"But your name shall be Abraham, for I have made you the father of a multitude of nations."

GENESIS 17:5 ESV

God has always loved to surprise us. A long time ago, He made a big promise to a man named Abraham. God told Abraham that one day his family would be so big, it would stretch across the whole world. But here was the problem: Abraham had no children. And most people thought he and his wife were too old to start a family. But they had faith—which means they believed God, even when it seemed impossible. And God kept His promise! Abraham and Sarah had a son, and today their descendants fill the world. God can do anything!

THOUGHT OF THE DAY

Can you think of some other promises God made to people in the Bible?

PRAY TODAY

Dear God, I love Your surprises! Help me remember to have faith in You, even when the things You promise seem impossible.

REAL PEACE

"I leave you peace. My peace I give you. I do not give it to you as the world does. So don't let your hearts be troubled."

JOHN 14:27 ICB

Do you know what peace is? It's a feeling of calmness and being sure that everything will be OK. But there are two kinds of peace: the kind that goes away when things get tough, and the kind that sticks around no matter that. The second kind is real peace, and that's what God promises to give you.

When things go wrong, or you feel angry, sad, or afraid, ask God to give you His gift of real peace. The things around you may not change, but God will change your heart. He'll help you find peace anywhere.

THOUGHT OF THE DAY

How do you think it feels to be peaceful?

PRAY TODAY

Dear God, when I feel upset, help me remember to ask for Your gift of peace. Amen.

OVER AND OVER AGAIN

"Rebuke your brother if he sins, and forgive him if he is sorry. Even if he wrongs you seven times a day and each time turns again and asks forgiveness, forgive him."

LUKE 17:3–4 TLB

There are no limits on God's forgiveness. He will always welcome us back into His arms and let us try again, over and over. Doesn't that feel great?

God says that we should forgive others in the same way. It's not easy! You might not feel like forgiving a classmate who hurts your feelings or a sister who ruins your art project. Especially if it keeps happening. But God doesn't want you to limit your forgiveness. So ask for His help. He can give you the strength and courage to forgive others over and over again.

THOUGHT OF THE DAY

How does it feel to be forgiven?

PRAY TODAY

Dear God, it isn't always easy to forgive, but I can do it with Your help. Help me forgive over and over, just like You do. Amen.

SEVENTY TIMES SEVEN

Then Peter came to him and asked, "Lord, how often should I forgive someone who sins against me? Seven times?" "No, not seven times," Jesus replied, "but seventy times seven!"

MATTHEW 18:21–22 NLT

Forgiveness isn't always easy. True forgiveness means we let go of wanting to get back at the person who hurt us. That's important, because God doesn't want feelings of anger to keep growing inside you. But it doesn't always happen right away.

So what if you try to forgive someone but that feeling doesn't go away? Should you give up? No! God says you should try until you get it right! You don't have to do it alone. Ask God for His help to forgive others the right way. Then keep trying. When true forgiveness happens, you'll feel so much better!

THOUGHT OF THE DAY

Forgiveness is good for everyone!

PRAY TODAY

Dear God, please help me forgive the right way—even if it takes a few tries! Amen.

THE GIFT OF LOVE

"For this is how God loved the world: He gave his one and only Son, so that everyone who believes in him will not perish but have eternal life."

JOHN 3:16 NLT

Sometimes we show our love for others by giving gifts. You might pick a big bouquet of flowers for your parents or spend your allowance to buy the perfect birthday present for your best friend. When you love someone, you want them to know!

God loves us so much, so He sent the most wonderful gift: Jesus. Jesus showed us what God's goodness looks like. He healed the sick, cared for the lonely, and invited everyone to be in God's family. Then He died and rose again so that we can all live in heaven with Him forever. What amazing love!

THOUGHT OF THE DAY

When you say a prayer of praise, it's like giving a gift back to God!

PRAY TODAY

Dear God, thank You for the wonderful gift of Jesus and for loving me so much! Amen.

YOU CAN TRUST HIM

"Do not be afraid or discouraged. For the LORD your God is with you wherever you go."

JOSHUA 1:9B NLT

Have you ever made a promise you couldn't keep? Has anyone ever broken a promise to you? When a promise is broken, it can be hard to trust that person again.

But do you know who never breaks a promise? God. And that's great news, because His promises are amazing! He says that He will give you rest. He'll be with you wherever you go. Nothing can separate you from His love. And through Jesus, He's promised you eternal life. You can feel good about trusting God. He always tells the truth, and He always keeps His promises.

THOUGHT OF THE DAY

God's promises are always true. Trusting Him is the thing to do!

PRAY TODAY

Dear God, thank You for keeping all Your wonderful promises. I'm glad I can trust You! Amen.

LAST OR FIRST

"So you want first place? Then take the last place. Be the servant of all."

MARK 9:35 MSG

When most people think about being first, they think about feeling like the most important person in the room. Maybe they get there by winning a trophy or having the most toys or being the line leader. But according to Jesus, none of that matters. Instead, to be first in God's kingdom, He says we should put ourselves last. That means helping and encouraging others, even if it slows us down or allows someone else to get more attention. When you do that, you make God smile. And that's the only first place prize that matters!

THOUGHT OF THE DAY

Can you find a way to put someone else first today?

PRAY TODAY

Dear God, I like being first. Please help me remember that to be first in Your eyes, I need to put myself last. Amen.

DAY 308

HIS VERY OWN

Long ago, even before he made the world, God chose us to be his very own through what Christ would do for us. . . . And he did this because he wanted to!

EPHESIANS 1:4–5 TLB

God loves you. You might already know that, but did you know that He loved you even before you were born? The Bible says God loved you even before the world began! He knew who you would be, and He wanted you to be part of His family. You are important to God.

You might feel upset or frustrated sometimes. Maybe you even wish you could change certain things about yourself. But God loves you just the way you are. He chose you to be His very own, and He'll never change His mind.

THOUGHT OF THE DAY

God chose you—so you are wonderful!

PRAY TODAY

Dear God, Your love makes me so happy! Thank You! Amen.

TRY GOING SECOND

"Greater love has no one than this: to lay down one's life for one's friends."

JOHN 15:13 NIV

God gives us an easy trick to being a great friend: let others go first. It's fun to be the line leader or the person who chooses what to play at recess. But try letting someone else go before you, and watch what happens. First, you'll make that person feel great. Everyone likes to feel important! Second, you might learn something new. Maybe your friend's funny idea will turn into your new favorite game! And third, YOU will feel great, because being kind is good for your heart. Ask God where you can go second today!

THOUGHT OF THE DAY

How does it feel to go first? Who can you give that feeling today?

PRAY TODAY

Dear God, please show me when I can give someone the gift of going first. Amen.

DAY 310

FIRST PLACE

For God has not given us a spirit of fear and timidity, but of power, love, and self-discipline.

2 TIMOTHY 1:7 NLT

Do you feel like faster is better? Some people rush around because they're afraid to miss out on anything. But God has enough good things for everyone! Being first isn't important to God—He's interested in HOW you do things, not how fast you do them. Did you check to make sure your chores were done well? Did you walk carefully to get in line, so you didn't bump into anyone? Did you listen well to a friend's story before you told your own? It's not always easy to slow down or wait your turn. But when you do, you take first place in God's eyes!

THOUGHT OF THE DAY

Take your time and you will see: there's plenty of good for you and me!

PRAY TODAY

Dear God, I really like to be first. Please help me know when it's better to slow down and take turns. Amen.

SIGNS OF LOVE

But if we love one another, God dwells deeply within us, and his love becomes complete in us—perfect love!

1 JOHN 4:12B MSG

God loves you, and He leaves signs of His love all around you. He has given you a beautiful world. Just look at the sunset each night! He listens to your prayers. Think of how He gives you courage to try new things or calms your nervous heart when you're afraid. And most of all, He gives you other people to love. When you love others, you are feeling God's love inside you. God's love covers your whole life. No matter where you go, you can't get away from it!

THOUGHT OF THE DAY

We love others because God loved us first!

PRAY TODAY

Dear God, thank You for loving every part of me! Amen.

KINDNESS HELPS EVERYONE!

A kind person is doing himself a favor.

PROVERBS 11:17A ICB

When you think about kindness, you probably think about doing something nice for someone else. But kindness is good for you too! Especially when it means making a new friend.

When you invite someone to play with you, you are showing kindness to him or her. It feels so good to be included! And the bonus is, you're also showing kindness to yourself. Everyone has great ideas. Maybe this new friend can help you make up a brand-new game. Maybe you can help each other build a super-tall sand castle, or climb a tricky tree! Showing kindness is the perfect way to start a friendship.

THOUGHT OF THE DAY

Next time you're playing, look around. Is there someone who might like to be included?

PRAY TODAY

Dear God, I want to be kind. Help me notice who is left out, and invite them to be my new friends! Amen.

MAKE GOOD CHOICES

Finally, brothers, whatever is true, whatever is honorable, whatever is just, whatever is pure, whatever is lovely, whatever is commendable, if there is any excellence, if there is anything worthy of praise, think about these things.

PHILIPPIANS 4:8 ESV

What kind of books and movies do you like? What do you talk about with your friends? The Bible says the things you think about can shape your attitudes and feelings. Some books and movies help us enjoy life and encourage us to help others. But some can make us feel worried or angry. We can talk with friends in kind ways, or we can gossip and spread rumors. God wants us to make choices that will lead to good attitudes. Ask Him to help you spend your time—and thoughts—wisely!

THOUGHT OF THE DAY

Reading Bible stories each day is a great way to fill your thoughts with good things!

PRAY TODAY

Dear God, help me spend time on things that will make me happy and kind. Amen.

KEEP GOING!

Noah was another who trusted God. When he heard God's warning about the future, Noah believed him even though there was then no sign of a flood, and wasting no time, he built the ark and saved his family.

HEBREWS 11:7 TLB

The story of Noah is exciting. With an enormous ship, he saved his whole family—and two of every kind of animal—from a dangerous flood!

But for a long time, Noah's life wasn't very exciting at all. Building that ship was hard work. His friends and neighbors thought his work was silly—it sure didn't seem like a flood was coming soon! Noah was probably lonely and discouraged a lot of the time. But he decided to trust God anyway. He kept working, and when the flood came, he was ready—just like God had promised!

THOUGHT OF THE DAY

What's hard for you right now? Do you think God can help you keep going?

PRAY TODAY

Dear God, please help me trust You like Noah did. With Your help, I can do anything! Amen.

DAY 315

GOD'S NEXT STEPS

A man's heart plans his way, but the Lord determines his steps.

PROVERBS 16:9 HCSB

It's so much fun to think about what you'll do when you grow up. Will you become someone famous? Or invent something brand-new? Maybe you'll write books, or visit faraway places, or build houses, or have kids of your own! Everyone has different dreams. That's why the world is such an interesting place!

Do you have big dreams? Ask God to help you take steps toward your goal. You might not always know what to do next, but God does! He can help you become exactly the person He's made you to be.

THOUGHT OF THE DAY

Make big plans, and don't forget that God knows every best next step!

PRAY TODAY

Dear God, You know what I want in my heart. Please guide my steps so I can do big things for You! Amen.

DAY 316

GREAT TEACHERS

No one in this world always does right.

ECCLESIASTES 7:20 CEV

Everyone makes mistakes. Some mistakes are small—like hitting the wrong key when you're learning to play piano. Some mistakes are bigger, like when you hurt a friend's feelings. But all mistakes have one thing in common: they are great teachers! Wrong notes sound funny, and that helps you find the right ones instead. Wrong choices can make you feel icky, and that helps you make the right choice next time. Don't get discouraged! God doesn't expect you to be perfect. He loves to help you learn from your mistakes so you can grow wiser and kinder each day.

THOUGHT OF THE DAY

How does it feel when you make a mistake?

PRAY TODAY

Dear God, sometimes I feel frustrated when I make mistakes, but I'm so glad You can help me learn from them! Amen.

LEADERS NEED PRAYERS TOO!

Pray for rulers and for all who have authority so that we can have quiet and peaceful lives full of worship and respect for God.

1 TIMOTHY 2:2 NCV

Who are some leaders you know about? You might think about someone famous, like a king or a president, but there are lots of leaders right in your community too. What about teachers, pastors, counselors, and parents? Every leader makes important decisions that affect others. So they all need God's guidance and wisdom! And you can make a difference by praying for your leaders. Ask God to help each one be honest, kind, and wise. Pray for peace and fairness everywhere. When you pray for powerful people, God can do powerful things!

THOUGHT OF THE DAY

What kind of leader would you be?

PRAY TODAY

Dear God, sometimes I forget that powerful people need prayers too. Please let those who lead us know Your wisdom and love. Amen.

GOD ANSWERS

"Then you will call upon Me and go and pray to Me, and I will listen to you."

JEREMIAH 29:12 NKJV

God wants you to pray about anything. He wants to hear what you're wondering about, excited about, and worried about. And when you ask Him things, He promises to answer! But God's answers don't always come the way you expect. You can't always hear God, like you can hear another person. God can answer prayers by giving you new ideas, or by calming your nervous feelings, or even through wise words someone else says to you! Keep praying and ask for help to notice His answers when they come. Remember that He loves you and is always with you.

THOUGHT OF THE DAY

God loves to hear and answer your prayers.

PRAY TODAY

Dear God, I love to talk to You. Help me be patient while I wait for Your answers. Amen.

PLENTY TO SHARE

And God will generously provide all you need. Then you will always have everything you need and plenty left over to share with others.

2 CORINTHIANS 9:8 NLT

God has promised to give us everything we need. But do you ever forget that? Sometimes it's hard to trust God. We might think we need more and more stuff to make us happy. But that's not true!

One way to get back to trusting God is to share what you have with others. Do you have a coat that's too small? Give it to a younger friend or sibling. What about books you don't read anymore? Can you donate them to your school? The more you give, the more you'll realize that God's given you all you need. In fact, He's given you plenty to share as well!

THOUGHT OF THE DAY

Choose one thing today that you can give away to someone who needs it.

PRAY TODAY

Dear God, please help me remember that You will give me everything I need. Then help me share with others! Amen.

YOU'VE GOT THIS!

"Don't worry about this Philistine," David told Saul. "I'll go fight him!"

1 SAMUEL 17:32 NLT

The Bible tells a story of a young boy named David who fought a huge warrior named Goliath. Everyone in the Israelite army was too afraid to fight Goliath, but David said, "I'll do it!" David wasn't even a soldier! But because he trusted God and used the talents God gave him, David won.

Hopefully, you'll never fight a giant! But maybe you have to do something else that takes courage, like perform in front of lots of people, or go to a new school. When something is scary, trust God to help you. He can make you brave like David!

THOUGHT OF THE DAY

God wants you to try big things. Trust in Him and the courage He brings!

PRAY TODAY

Dear God, sometimes I just don't want to do scary things. Help me trust in You, just like David did. Amen.

WHAT'S HAPPENING?

"I know that You can do all things. Nothing can put a stop to Your plans."

JOB 42:2 NLV

Do you ever wonder about what is going to happen in the future? What you'll be when you grow up? If you'll have great adventures?

Because we are human, we don't know the future. But there is one thing we can be sure about: God knows all about it. God has good plans, and nothing can stop them. When you wonder about how things will turn out, remember to pray and thank God that His good plans will come to pass. You can rest, knowing that God is in control of today—and tomorrow too!

THOUGHT OF THE DAY

You may not know the future, but you can know it is in God's hands.

PRAY TODAY

Dear God, I'm so thankful that You know all about the future. Thank You for Your good plans. Amen.

COUNT ON GOD'S GOODNESS

Surely goodness and mercy shall follow me all the days of my life, and I shall dwell in the house of the LORD forever.

PSALM 23:6 ESV

The Bible tells us that God is good. Does that mean that only good things happen to people? No. Sometimes bad things happen. People get sick. People get hurt. Things don't always turn out the way we would like.

But that doesn't mean that God is not good. God never leaves us. God always helps us, even when bad things happen. God comforts us. He sends friends and family to share His love with us. He can even bring good things out of bad times! You can always count on God, because He is always good!

THOUGHT OF THE DAY

What are some ways God has shown His goodness to you?

PRAY TODAY

Dear God, thank You for always being good. I'm so glad I can always count on Your love for me. Amen.

THANK YOU, GOD

Praise the LORD. Give thanks to the LORD, for he is good; his love endures forever.

PSALM 106:1 NIV

How do you feel when you give someone a present, but they don't say thanks? If you help someone, but they never even take time to thank you, how does it make you feel?

Think about all the wonderful gifts God gives you every day—family, friends, answered prayers, a home, and all of nature. You are God's beloved child, and He loves to give you good things. He also loves to know that you are thankful. Be sure to take time each day to give thanks to the Lord.

THOUGHT OF THE DAY

What are some things you want to thank God for today?

PRAY TODAY

Dear God, thank You for all Your amazing and good gifts. I love You. Amen.

LEARN TO LAUGH

"He will yet fill your mouth with laughter, and your lips with shouting."

JOB 8:21 ESV

Bob and Larry love to tell jokes. Here's a good one: What was the only animal Noah couldn't trust to play fair? The cheetah! Here's another: Why couldn't they play card games on the ark? Because Noah was always standing on the deck!

Telling funny jokes and being silly is just fine with God. He loves to hear us laugh. Some people think that God wants us to be serious all the time. But that's not what the Bible says. When you're happy, laugh. When you feel silly, giggle. Let others know that "God has filled your mouth with laughter!"

THOUGHT OF THE DAY

What makes you laugh? Do you have a favorite VeggieTales silly song that you like to sing?

PRAY TODAY

Dear God, I love to laugh. Please help me bring joy to others too. Amen.

GOD'S SURPRISES

"Do you think you can explain the mystery of God? Do you think you can diagram God Almighty? God is far higher than you can imagine, far deeper than you can comprehend."

JOB 11:7–8 MSG

Has God ever surprised you? Maybe something wonderful happened that you weren't expecting! Or maybe you didn't get what you wanted. God's surprises can be exciting, disappointing, or just plain confusing! But never forget: God knows best. God loves you. And He has amazing plans for you!

When things don't happen the way you hoped, ask God to help you find and share joy in every situation. You may feel disappointed, but keep trusting God. His plans are even greater than you can imagine!

THOUGHT OF THE DAY

We can't understand everything about God. But we can understand that He loves us.

PRAY TODAY

Dear God, please help me remember that Your plan is best, even when it's not what I expected! Amen.

TRUST GOD

Commit everything you do to the LORD. Trust him, and he will help you.

PSALM 37:5 NLT

God says that we can always trust Him. That means when God makes a promise, He keeps it.

And one of the best promises He's made is to help His children—with everything! Have you ever felt scared? Ask God to take away your fear. Are you learning something new? Pray for the patience to keep trying. Are you lonely? Ask Him to bring good friends your way! Talk to God anytime, about anything. When you trust God, He can help you. It's what He loves to do!

THOUGHT OF THE DAY

How do you know God loves you? Did He say it? Then it's true!

PRAY TODAY

Dear God, I'm so glad I can trust You. Help me remember to ask for Your help when I am having a hard time. Amen.

GOD'S SPECIAL LANGUAGE

"My sheep hear My voice, I know them, and they follow Me."

JOHN 10:27 HCSB

Have you ever noticed grown-ups talking about "hearing God's voice"? That's a little confusing, because most of the time, we don't hear God like we hear other people! Instead, God uses other ways to talk to us.

God likes to give us good thoughts that are hard to ignore. Do you have an idea for helping others? Do you find that you can't stop thinking about inviting the new kid to play or apologizing for a mistake you made? Sometimes God speaks by giving us courage when we need to do something hard or scary. Pay attention to God's special language. When you do, you'll "hear" great things!

THOUGHT OF THE DAY

You hear God best when you listen with your heart.

PRAY TODAY

Dear God, I want to hear Your voice. Help me pay attention with my heart so I'll always know what You're saying! Amen.

DAY 328

JESUS LOVES YOU!

"You're blessed when you're content with just who you are—no more, no less."

MATTHEW 5:5A MSG

God loves everything about you. No one else does things exactly like you do them or has exactly your ideas. No one else can love your family and friends like you can. The world needs you! You're amazing!

But you might not always feel amazing. You might wish you looked different, or thought differently, or were more like someone else. When you start feeling that way, remember that Jesus loves you right now. Not you with different hair or a quieter voice or more friends or bigger toys. He loves you just as you are. And you should love you too!

THOUGHT OF THE DAY

What are three things you love about yourself?

PRAY TODAY

Dear God, I am Your special creation. Thank You for making me just the way I am. Amen.

HOW WOULD YOU LIKE IT?

"Just as you want others to do for you, do the same for them."

LUKE 6:31 HCSB

The Bible says we should treat others the way we'd like to be treated. So let's play a game. Imagine you're playing with two friends—one uses good manners and the other uses no manners at all. Which one would let you go first or say "I'm sorry" if she made a mistake? What kinds of words would each friend say if he or she didn't get his or her way? And which friend would you like to play with again tomorrow?

Next time you're with friends, remember the two pretend ones you imagined today. Then act like the friend you'd like to have!

THOUGHT OF THE DAY

Use good manners—you can't go wrong! You'll show kindness all day long.

PRAY TODAY

Dear God, please help me remember good manners so I will always treat others with kindness. Amen.

A GREAT BIG FAMILY

"And I will be a father to you, and you shall be sons and daughters to me, says the Lord Almighty."

2 CORINTHIANS 6:18 ESV

A loving family is one of God's greatest gifts. When the people in a family care for and support each other, home feels like the safest, happiest place in the world.

And guess what? We are all part of God's family! He's our loving parent, cheering us on, holding us when we're scared, and helping us learn and grow every day.

Do you know someone who doesn't have a happy family? Look for ways to be a loving sister to them. Then they can feel happily at home as part of God's great big family!

THOUGHT OF THE DAY

Who lives at your house? Is your family big or small?

PRAY TODAY

Dear God, thank You for the gift of my family! Help me act like a good sister to others. Amen.

GOOD WORK IS HARD WORK

So let's not get tired of doing what is good. At just the right time we will reap a harvest of blessing if we don't give up.

GALATIANS 6:9 NLT

Sometimes doing the right thing means saying yes—to helping out with chores or sharing what you have. Sometimes it means saying no—to selfishness and unkind words. It's not always easy to make the right choice. You might even get tired of doing what's good—especially if no one seems to pay attention! But don't give up! God sees you making good choices and He knows you're working hard. He loves to see you thinking about your words, helping a sibling, or spending your time with someone who feels left out. So keep going! God is cheering you on!

THOUGHT OF THE DAY

Are good choices ever hard for you? Talk to your parents! Maybe they have some ideas to help.

PRAY TODAY

Dear God, sometimes it's easier to make the wrong choice. Help me to be strong so I can choose good things all the time! Amen.

GOD'S GOT THIS

Since God assured us, "I'll never let you down, never walk off and leave you," we can boldly quote, "God is there, ready to help; I'm fearless no matter what. Who or what can get to me?"

HEBREWS 13:5–6 MSG

Did you know that God is the answer to every problem? No matter what you're facing, God can help.

Sometimes just talking to God can help you feel better. Praying for courage or peace is a great way to overcome fears! God often works through people and will provide helpers like parents or friends to guide you. And other times, God will give you an idea for a solution to try! There are so many different ways He can help us. But one thing's always true: nothing is too hard for God!

THOUGHT OF THE DAY

Is there something you need help with today? Talk to God about it!

PRAY TODAY

Dear God, please help me when I feel discouraged. I'm so glad nothing is too hard for You. Amen.

DAY 333

SPEAK GENTLY

Always be humble, gentle, and patient, accepting each other in love.

EPHESIANS 4:2 NCV

Do you ever have a hard time being quiet? Maybe you love to talk first—or loudest—to make sure everyone hears you. And when you have something interesting to say, it's hard to wait your turn!

The Bible tells us to be gentle with each other. You probably know to be gentle with your actions, but it's important that your words are gentle too. Speaking gently means you choose kind, helpful words. It means being patient when others are speaking and paying attention too. When you listen carefully, you can respond with wisdom, care, and your own great ideas!

THOUGHT OF THE DAY

Words can be as powerful as actions—use both gently!

PRAY TODAY

Dear God, thank You for giving me good ideas. Help me be patient, pay attention, and use my words to help! Amen.

TALK ABOUT IT

"Those who are sad now are happy. God will comfort them."

MATTHEW 5:4 ICB

No one can be happy all day every day. We all feel sad sometimes, and that's OK!

But don't be sad all by yourself. Talk to someone! God cares about your feelings, and He's given you loving people who are ready to listen. Your parents know you best, and maybe they've felt some of the same feelings you have. A good friend can also listen and encourage you. Teachers, grandparents, and siblings can be great listeners too. And don't forget that you can talk to God anytime you want to. In fact, He's the best place to start!

THOUGHT OF THE DAY

Happy or sad, you are never alone. God loves you!

PRAY TODAY

Dear God, please help me remember to talk to You when I'm sad. Then help me talk to others who love me too. Amen.

BELIEVE IN YOURSELF

"Don't be afraid. Only believe."

MARK 5:36B HCSB

Can you think of a time you tried something new? Sometimes new things feel scary. But when you trust Jesus, you don't need to be afraid. And in today's verse, Jesus even gives you the secret to trusting Him: just believe!

When you feel nervous to try something new, remember and believe the things Jesus says: He loves you, He'll never leave you, and He's given you good gifts. Then jump in and do your best! You won't do things perfectly at first—no one does! Just remind yourself of Jesus' promises, learn from your mistakes, and try again. Your next new thing might become your new favorite thing!

THOUGHT OF THE DAY

Is there something new you want to try? Ask Jesus to help you learn!

PRAY TODAY

Dear Jesus, I believe that You are always with me. Please give me courage and patience to try new things! Amen.

BLOW YOUR WORRIES AWAY!

Give all your worries and cares to God, for he cares about you.

1 PETER 5:7 NLT

Have you ever felt worried? Worry happens when you can't stop thinking about a problem. God doesn't want you to spend all your energy worrying about things. Instead, He says to give your worries to Him!

How can you do that? A fun way to picture it is by blowing bubbles. Imagine that each bubble has a worry inside it. Then, watch them float up, up, and away. Ask God to take each worry and get rid of it. As the bubbles pop or disappear into the sky, thank God for lifting your worries from your mind.

THOUGHT OF THE DAY

Fill your mind with God each day. He can carry your cares away!

PRAY TODAY

Dear God, thank You for caring about me. Please take my worries away! Amen.

QUEEN OF KINDNESS

If you really keep the royal law found in Scripture, "Love your neighbor as yourself," you are doing right.

JAMES 2:8 NIV

Have you ever wanted to be a queen? When you follow God's Word, you can! The Bible tells us that when you treat others the way you'd like to be treated, you are following a "royal law." When you listen well and help friends solve problems, you're like King Solomon, who was full of wisdom. When you stand up for others who are in trouble, you're like Queen Esther, whose spoke up and saved her people from an evil plot. Each day, find ways to put others first. You will be royally blessed!

THOUGHT OF THE DAY

What's something kind you'd like to hear from a friend? Say that to someone today!

PRAY TODAY

Dear God, help me remember to treat everyone with kindness and respect. I know we are all precious to You! Amen.

DAY 338

FOLLOW YOUR HEART

Finally, all of you should be of one mind. Sympathize with each other. Love each other as brothers and sisters. Be tenderhearted, and keep a humble attitude.

1 PETER 3:8 NLT

Think of someone you love. How do you like to treat them? Most of us are kind to the people we love. And that's good!

But God wants us to show kindness to everyone—including those we don't know or even get along with! That's a little harder, but here's a trick: check with your heart! Do you have a feeling inside that you should invite a new neighbor to your birthday party? Or stop sharing gossip? Or donate some of your allowance to help hungry people eat? That's your heart helping you find kindness. So follow your heart! Kindness is always the best choice.

THOUGHT OF THE DAY

Kindness starts in your heart—but it doesn't stop there!

PRAY TODAY

Dear God, please show me how to be kind to everyone! Amen.

ALWAYS TOGETHER

"I assure you: Anyone who believes has eternal life."

JOHN 6:47 HCSB

God loves you so much. He never wants to be apart from You. And that's why He sent Jesus! Because of Jesus, everyone who wants to can be with God forever. What wonderful news!

When you invite Jesus to live in your heart, He stays there forever. You can never make a mistake bad enough to make Him leave. Nothing you say or do—and nothing you've said or done before—can keep you from God, and no one can take Him away from you. You will always be part of God's family. That's a promise you can count on!

THOUGHT OF THE DAY

God loves you—yesterday, today, and always!

PRAY TODAY

Dear God, I am so glad Your love is forever! Amen.

FILLED WITH GRACE

For by grace you have been saved through faith. And this is not your own doing; it is the gift of God.

EPHESIANS 2:8 ESV

Sometimes you get a reward for doing something well—like a trophy for winning a race. But you can have God's grace without doing anything at all! It's free, and it's the best gift ever.

Grace means God cares for us, no matter what we do. And He loves us so much, He sent Jesus to save us. God's grace is for anyone who wants it! You don't have to wonder if you're "good enough." You don't have to work extra hard and hope that he chooses you. All you have to do is accept—and enjoy!—His wonderful gift.

THOUGHT OF THE DAY

You are enough for God, just because you're YOU.

PRAY TODAY

Dear God, thank You so much for Your grace. I love knowing I'm Your child forever. Amen.

YOU CAN DO ANYTHING

Jesus said to him . . . "Everything is possible to the one who believes."

MARK 9:23 HCSB

God promises to help you do great things when you trust Him. You don't have to be afraid to try something new—with God's help, you can do anything!

That doesn't mean everything will be easy. You may have to work hard to learn new things. It'll take courage to make new friends. You'll have to practice before you can play your instrument well or kick that winning soccer goal or draw a perfect spaceship. But God gives you strength, perseverance, and joy along the way! So don't give up. After all, God will never give up on you.

THOUGHT OF THE DAY

Believe in God, and He'll help you believe in yourself!

PRAY TODAY

Dear God, sometimes I get discouraged. Please help me remember that with You, I can do anything! Amen.

DAY 342

WHOSE CHILD ARE YOU?

Dear friends, let us practice loving each other, for love comes from God and those who are loving and kind show that they are the children of God, and that they are getting to know him better.

1 JOHN 4:7 TLB

How do you show that you belong to your family? Do you look like your parents or your brothers or sisters? Do you all have the same last name? Do you all live in the same place?

We are all part of God's family. And the Bible tells us that there's a special way we can show it: be kind and loving! Look for ways to help others, share with them, listen to them, and be a good friend. When you do this, you're showing the world who your Heavenly Father is!

THOUGHT OF THE DAY

How will you show someone you are in God's family today?

PRAY TODAY

Dear God, thank You for making me part of Your family. Please help me to practice loving others so they know I love You! Amen.

PUT OUT THE FIRE

Without wood, a fire will go out, and without gossip, quarreling will stop.

PROVERBS 26:20 NCV

Do you know what keeps a fire burning? Wood! If there is no more wood, a fire will go out. Today's Bible verse says that quarreling—or arguing—is like a burning fire. When we gossip, or talk about others in unkind ways, it is like tossing more and more wood on a fire. It makes an argument get bigger and bigger. But if someone stops saying unkind or mean things, then the arguing stops. You can be a good friend and help put out "fiery" quarrels by using kind words instead of gossip.

THOUGHT OF THE DAY

Kind words cool off hot tempers!

PRAY TODAY

Dear God, please help me to use my words carefully. Help me say kind things instead of gossip. Amen.

DO IT FOR JESUS!

"... I tell you the truth, anything you did for even the least of my people here, you also did for me."

MATTHEW 25:40 NCV

Sometimes it's hard to put others first. But what if you imagine that you're actually serving Jesus? The Bible tells us that when we do something kind for someone else, it's as if we're doing it for Jesus! So when your sister begs you to share your toys, imagine it's Jesus sitting there. Try to see Him in everyone you meet—the new kid at school who looks lonely at recess, the older folks at church you could hold the door open for, or the homeless person who might need food. Showing kindness to other people is a great way to love Jesus.

THOUGHT OF THE DAY

How can you show kindness to someone new today?

PRAY TODAY

Dear Jesus, please help me remember that loving You means loving others too. Amen.

GOD'S GOOD GIFTS

Every good gift and every perfect gift is from above, and comes down from the Father of lights.

JAMES 1:17 NKJV

Don't you love receiving gifts? Maybe you also love giving gifts to those you love. Do you know that God loves to give His children good and perfect gifts? God's perfect gifts aren't just for birthdays or Christmas, and they never wear out or break. They are wonderful things like the love of your family and friends, the majesty of a golden sunset, the beauty of a starry sky, the amazing way you grow and learn new things. Look around and remember to thank God for all the good and perfect gifts He gives you each day!

THOUGHT OF THE DAY

Name some of the good gifts God has given you!

PRAY TODAY

Dear God, thank You for loving me so much and for giving me good and perfect gifts every day. Amen.

SHOW AND TELL

Little children, let us stop just saying we love people; let us really love them, and show it by our actions.

1 JOHN 3:18 TLB

Have you heard of show-and-tell? It's when you bring something—maybe a favorite toy—to your class and talk about it. If you just told your class about your special toy, but you didn't show it, they wouldn't see it. But if you just showed it to them, and didn't say anything about it, they wouldn't know much about it. Love is like that. We need to both show and tell people that we love them. Words are important, but showing our love by helping, sharing, being kind, and forgiving helps people know how much we love them.

THOUGHT OF THE DAY

To love others well, show and tell!

PRAY TODAY

Dear God, please help me to use both my words and my actions to let others know I love them. Amen.

A NEW YOU

Put on the new self, created to be like God in true righteousness and holiness.

EPHESIANS 4:24 NIV

Do you ever say, "That's just the way I am! I can't change." It is easy to keep doing things the same old way. But did you know that the Bible says you can "put on a new self?" You don't have to always lose your temper. You don't have to always have your own way. If you want to, you can choose to be different. With God's help you can "put on a new self." Each morning, ask God to help you put on kindness, patience, and understanding. Then look for opportunities to practice being the new you!

THOUGHT OF THE DAY

What is one way you'd like to change and grow today?

PRAY TODAY

Dear God, sometimes I do or say things that aren't kind. Please help me to choose a different way. Amen.

WORKING TOGETHER

Two are better than one, because they get more done by working together.

ECCLESIASTES 4:9 NCV

What do you wish for when you have a big chore to do? A friend to help you out! What does your friend wish for when they have a problem to solve? You! When two buddies work together, they can get the job done in half the time. The work is easier, and then you both have more time to play! Look around. Is there someone who needs help? Lend them a hand. And when you have a job that seems tough to do, don't be afraid to ask for a little help. Working together is much better (and way more fun!) than working alone.

THOUGHT OF THE DAY

Who can you help today?

PRAY TODAY

Dear God, thank You for always helping me. Please remind me to work together with others! Amen.

LET'S SING!

Sing to the Lord a new song; sing to the Lord, all the earth. Sing to the Lord and praise his name; every day tell how he saves us.

PSALM 96:1–2 NCV

The Veggies love to sing songs—happy songs and silly songs, songs that tell stories and songs that make you want to dance! Do you know who else loves songs? God does! He loves to hear His children singing and making music. Singing is a great way to remind ourselves how much God loves us. Have you ever learned fun songs at Sunday school, church camp, or Vacation Bible School? Why not sing them? Or make up your own! It's a fun way to tell God know how much we love Him and how glad we are that He loves us too!

THOUGHT OF THE DAY

What song would you like to sing to God?

PRAY TODAY

Dear God, thank You for loving me. Please fill my heart with songs I can sing to You! Amen.

POWER TO SHARE

Do not withhold good from those who deserve it when it's in your power to help them.

PROVERBS 3:27 NLT

If you have a cookie and your friend has none, you could break your cookie in half and share it. If you have two toys and your buddy doesn't have one, you could share and play together. The Bible says that it's always good to give and share when we have something that others need. Sharing might feel hard to do, but it's actually a special power. It makes friendships stronger and helps others! You can use this special power any time you want—just look around and see if there's someone you can help. Then go save the day!

THOUGHT OF THE DAY

The power to share will show that you care.

PRAY TODAY

Dear God, I am so thankful for all You have given me. Please help me use my power to share with others. Amen.

YOUR BODY, GOD'S TEMPLE

Don't you know that you are God's temple and that God's Spirit lives in you?

1 CORINTHIANS 3:16 NCV

There are many things that make you special, but one of the most amazing is that God says you are His temple. A temple is the place where God lives. In Old Testament times, the temple was a building in Israel. But after Jesus returned to heaven, He sent His Spirit to live in each person who believes in Him. That makes your body God's temple! When you take care of your body you honor God. Eating good food, exercising, making safe choices, and getting enough rest are all good ways to take care of God's temple!

THOUGHT OF THE DAY

What are some ways you take care of your body?

PRAY TODAY

Thank You, God, for giving me such an amazing body. Help me to honor You by taking good care of it. Amen.

PRACTICE PATIENCE

But they that wait upon the LORD shall renew their strength; they shall mount up with wings as eagles; they shall run, and not be weary; and they shall walk, and not faint.

ISAIAH 40:31 KJV

Do you hate to wait? It's sometimes hard to be patient! Maybe you feel frustrated when the things you want to do seem too hard right now. God understands, and He gives you a wonderful promise. He says that if you will be patient, then at just the right time, He will help you do the things He created you to do. And even better, He will give you the strength to do them well! Trust that God is there to help you and be patient. You and God will do amazing things!

THOUGHT OF THE DAY

What is something you need to be patient about?

PRAY TODAY

Thank You, God, for helping me to grow. Please help me be patient as I wait for Your help. Amen.

FEELINGS

There is a right time for everything. . . . A time to cry; A time to laugh; A time to grieve; A time to dance.

ECCLESIASTES 3:1, 4 TLB

Everyone has feelings. You might feel happy one day and sad the next. Sometimes you feel like dancing and other times you feel like being quiet. God created us with the ability to feel different ways at different times. The Bible reminds us it's OK to have these feelings. And if our feelings ever seem too big to keep inside, we can talk to a parent or a friend. We can tell God about it too! It's good to share your feelings and to understand that no matter how you feel, God's love for you never changes.

THOUGHT OF THE DAY

God always loves you . . . no matter how you feel!

PRAY TODAY

Dear God, I'm glad You care about my feelings. Help me to remember that You love me all the time! Amen.

DAY 354

DOING HARD THINGS

"I say to you who are listening to me, love your enemies. Do good to those who hate you. Ask God to bless those who say bad things to you. Pray for those who are cruel to you."

LUKE 6:27–28 ICB

When Jesus taught people how to live, He sometimes asked them to do hard things. In our verse today, Jesus tells His friends to be kind and loving to people who are mean and hateful. That isn't easy. But Jesus knows that love is more powerful than hate, and kindness is greater than meanness. When we pray for and try to love those who treat us poorly, we are showing them God's way to live. And if we will do the hard things He asks us to do, Jesus can use us to shine His love in the world and even change people's lives!

THOUGHT OF THE DAY

How will you show love to someone today?

PRAY TODAY

Dear God, I want to do the hard things You ask me to do. Please help me to be kind and loving today. Amen.

CHOOSE TO TRUST GOD

When I am afraid, I will trust in You.

PSALM 56:3 HCSB

Did you know that everyone feels afraid sometimes? Even teenagers and grownups feel afraid. Some of us are afraid of getting lost, or being alone, or not doing well in a game or at school. The world is a big place and there is so much we don't know. That's why the Bible reminds us to trust in God whenever we feel afraid. God made the world, and He created you too! He is greater than anything we fear. When we choose to trust in Him, He will calm our hearts and help us be less afraid.

THOUGHT OF THE DAY

Give your fears to God. He is big enough to take care of them!

PRAY TODAY

Dear God, I'm so glad You are greater than my fears! Help me to trust in You all the time! Amen.

BE A LIGHT-BRINGER

Walk as children of light (for the fruit of light is found in all that is good and right and true).

EPHESIANS 5:8B–9 ESV

What does it mean to "walk as children of light"? Does it mean to wear shoes that glow in the dark? Does it mean to carry a flashlight around all the time? No! When the Bible says "walk as children of light," it means we should try to live in ways that please Jesus. Be kind. Say words that help people, not hurt them. Tell the truth. If someone does something that makes you mad, try to forgive. Speak up when you see something unfair. These kinds of things shine the light of Jesus into the world. So be a light-bringer wherever you go!

THOUGHT OF THE DAY

Can you sing "This Little Light of Mine"?

PRAY TODAY

Dear God, thank You for shining Your light on me. Help me to be a light-bringer everywhere I go today. Amen.

GOD ALWAYS FORGIVES

Those who hide their sins won't succeed, but those who confess and give them up will receive mercy.

PROVERBS 28:13 CEB

Have you ever done something wrong and then tried to cover it up? Maybe you told a lie, or you blamed someone else. But when you do that, you probably still feel afraid and worried that someone might find out. God says that when we do something wrong, we need to say we did it and ask to be forgiven. God loves to forgive His children. He wants you to learn from your mistakes and try again. You never have to be afraid to tell God what you've done wrong. He will always forgive you.

THOUGHT OF THE DAY

God loves to forgive His children.

PRAY TODAY

Dear God, I'm sorry for the times I've done things that were wrong. Thank You for loving and forgiving me. Amen.

DAY 358

SMALL BECOMES GREAT

"There's a youngster here with five barley loaves and a couple of fish! But what good is that with all this mob?"

JOHN 6:9 TLB

Once Jesus was teaching and a great crowd of people were listening. At dinnertime they were hungry, but they had no food. Then a boy gave Jesus his small lunch. Jesus prayed and a great miracle happened: suddenly there was enough food for everyone! Because the boy shared, everyone was blessed. You can share what you have too. Even if you think it is something small, Jesus can use it to do great things! You can share your time, your help, your smiles, your snacks, or your toys. It may seem small, but Jesus can make it great!

THOUGHT OF THE DAY

What will you share today?

PRAY TODAY

Thank You, God, for Your many blessings. Please help me share what I have so You can use it to bless others. Amen.

DAY 359

GOD WILL HELP YOU

Commit everything you do to the LORD. Trust him, and he will help you.

PSALM 37:5 NLT

When you need to do something that is hard or scary, how do you feel? Do you worry? Do you whine? Do you get mad and refuse to do it? Going to a new class, visiting the dentist, staying overnight at grandma's house, and going on a trip are all things that might seem hard. But God says He will help you if you trust Him. You can tell Him about your feelings and He will give you courage, calm your fears, and help you do hard things. God always loves to help you. All you have to do is ask!

THOUGHT OF THE DAY

When was a time God helped you do something hard?

PRAY TODAY

Dear God, I'm so glad You are always ready to help me. Thank You for loving me so much. Amen.

CHOOSE WHAT'S GOOD

I can do anything I want to if Christ has not said no, but some of these things aren't good for me.

1 CORINTHIANS 6:12A TLB

You make choices every day. Some choices are between what's right and wrong. But other choices are about what's good for you. You need to sleep, but it isn't good for you to stay in bed all day. It's important to eat, but not so great to eat only cookies. It's fine to have toys, but it's not good to beg and whine to get more and more toys. A wise person learns to choose what is good. The next time you make a choice, remember to ask God if it is a good choice.

THOUGHT OF THE DAY

What is a good choice you can make today?

PRAY TODAY

Thank You, God, for what You've given me. Help me to always choose what is good for me. Amen.

A LITTLE FAITH

"Truly I tell you, if you have faith as small as a mustard seed, you can say to this mountain, 'Move from here to there,' and it will move. Nothing will be impossible for you."

MATTHEW 17:20B NIV

Sometimes people think that bigger means better. You can buy super-sized sodas and giant packs of cereal or cookies. There's even a place where you can buy a beach ball as tall as your ceiling! But did you know that the Bible says you only need a small bit of faith to do amazing things? It's true. Do you know why? It's because your faith is in our great God. When you trust and believe in Him, you are counting on God's power, not your own. And God can do all things. He is bigger—and better—than anything!

THOUGHT OF THE DAY

Small faith + a great God = miracles!

PRAY TODAY

I'm so glad that You are such a great God! Thank You for taking my small faith and doing wonderful things! Amen.

CLIMB INTO JOY

A cheerful heart does good like medicine.

PROVERBS 17:22A TLB

Feeling grumpy is no fun. Some people call it being "down in the dumps." But building a cheerful heart makes it easier to climb out of those dumpy, grumpy feelings!

So how do you get a cheerful heart? Every day, find something to be happy about. It can be something small like a pretty flower, or something big like a birthday party. When you build the good habit of seeing God's blessings all around you, your heart will get used to being cheerful. Then on grumpy days, your cheerful heart will boost you out of the dumps!

THOUGHT OF THE DAY

What made you feel cheerful today?

PRAY TODAY

Dear God, thank You for Your wonderful world. Please help me find reasons to be cheerful each day! Amen.

GOD'S GIFT TO YOU

This is the day the LORD has made; let us rejoice and be glad in it.

PSALM 118:24 ESV

Do you know that God gives you a gift every day? What about today? What will happen? Who will you see? Beginning a fresh new day is a little like opening a present! So why not start the day by thanking God for it? Tell Him how glad you are for everything He has given you: a body so you can enjoy the world, a mind so you can think and dream, the rain and sunshine, plants and animals, friends and family. Every new day comes from God, and He wants you to enjoy it!

THOUGHT OF THE DAY

At the start of each new day, give thanks to God, rejoice, and pray!

PRAY TODAY

Thank You, God, for making this day. I'm so glad You love me and want me to be filled with joy! Amen.

REMEMBER TO TELL THE TRUTH

Don't ever forget kindness and truth. Wear them like a necklace. Write them on your heart as if on a tablet.

PROVERBS 3:3 NCV

Sometimes it is hard to tell the truth. Maybe you did something you knew was wrong, and you were afraid you would get in trouble. Maybe you don't want to tell the truth because someone might make fun of you. But telling the truth is so important that God says to "wear the truth like a necklace" and "write truth on your heart." Those are word pictures that mean we should be honest wherever we go. Give it a try. When you practice telling the truth, it becomes easier and easier to do.

THOUGHT OF THE DAY

Practice telling the truth today in everything you do and say!

PRAY TODAY

Dear God, thank You for Your words of truth in the Bible. Help me be a person who remembers to tell the truth. Amen.

GOD IS THERE TO HELP

Depend on the Lord and his strength. Always go to him for help.

1 CHRONICLES 16:11 ICB

Isn't it great when a friend helps you solve a problem or learn something new? Doesn't it feel good to know that your parents are there to help you when you don't know what to do? God is a good friend and Father, and He wants to help you too. God has more wisdom and strength than any person in the world, and He is always there, even when you feel alone. The Bible tells us that when we take our problems to God, He is happy to help us.

THOUGHT OF THE DAY

What is something you will ask God to help you with today?

PRAY TODAY

Dear God, I'm so glad You are always there to help me. Thank You for loving me so much. Amen.

KNOW IT BY HEART

MOM OR DAD, HELP YOUR DAUGHTER MEMORIZE THIS VERSE AND TALK TO HER ABOUT WHAT IT MEANS.

But the fruit of the Spirit is love, joy, peace, patience, kindness, goodness, faithfulness, gentleness, self-control; against such things there is no law.

GALATIANS 5:22–23 NASB

KNOW IT BY HEART

MOM OR DAD, HELP YOUR DAUGHTER MEMORIZE THIS VERSE AND TALK TO HER ABOUT WHAT IT MEANS.

"Fear not, for I am with you."

ISAIAH 43:5A ESV

KNOW IT BY HEART

MOM OR DAD, HELP YOUR DAUGHTER MEMORIZE THIS VERSE AND TALK TO HER ABOUT WHAT IT MEANS.

How wonderful and pleasant it is
when brothers live together in harmony!

PSALM 133:1 NLT

KNOW IT BY HEART

MOM OR DAD, HELP YOUR DAUGHTER MEMORIZE THIS VERSE AND TALK TO HER ABOUT WHAT IT MEANS.

Give thanks to the Lord for He is good!
His loving-kindness lasts forever!

PSALM 107:1 NLV

KNOW IT BY HEART

MOM OR DAD, HELP YOUR DAUGHTER MEMORIZE THIS VERSE
AND TALK TO HER ABOUT WHAT IT MEANS.

*Follow God's example, therefore,
as dearly loved children.*

EPHESIANS 5:1 NIV

KNOW IT BY HEART

MOM OR DAD, HELP YOUR DAUGHTER MEMORIZE THIS VERSE
AND TALK TO HER ABOUT WHAT IT MEANS.

"I say this because I know what I am
planning for you," says the LORD.
"I have good plans for you,
not plans to hurt you.
I will give you hope and a good future."

JEREMIAH 29:11 NCV

KNOW IT BY HEART

MOM OR DAD, HELP YOUR DAUGHTER MEMORIZE THIS VERSE AND TALK TO HER ABOUT WHAT IT MEANS.

Rejoice in the Lord always.
Again I will say, rejoice!

PHILIPPIANS 4:4 NKJV

KNOW IT BY HEART

MOM OR DAD, HELP YOUR DAUGHTER MEMORIZE THIS VERSE
AND TALK TO HER ABOUT WHAT IT MEANS.

Put up with each other,
and forgive anyone who does you wrong,
just as Christ has forgiven you.

COLOSSIANS 3:13 CEV

KNOW IT BY HEART

MOM OR DAD, HELP YOUR DAUGHTER MEMORIZE THIS VERSE AND TALK TO HER ABOUT WHAT IT MEANS.

Jesus Christ is the same yesterday, today, and forever.

HEBREWS 13:8 TLB

KNOW IT BY HEART

MOM OR DAD, HELP YOUR DAUGHTER MEMORIZE THIS VERSE AND TALK TO HER ABOUT WHAT IT MEANS.

The man who gives much will have much,
and he who helps others
will be helped himself.

PROVERBS 11:25 NLV

KNOW IT BY HEART

MOM OR DAD, HELP YOUR DAUGHTER MEMORIZE THIS VERSE
AND TALK TO HER ABOUT WHAT IT MEANS.

Love the LORD your God
with all your heart and with all your soul
and with all your strength.

DEUTERONOMY 6:5 NIV